REDEMPTION IN
GENESIS

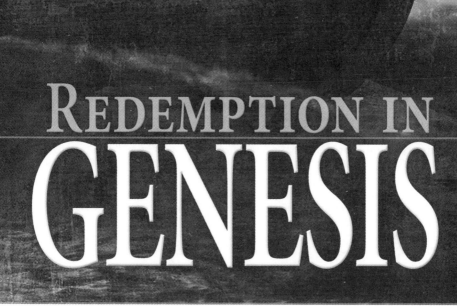

REDEMPTION IN
GENESIS

THE CROSSROADS OF FAITH AND REASON

JOHN S. NIXON

Pacific Press® Publishing Association
Nampa, Idaho
Oshawa, Ontario, Canada
www.pacificpress.com

Cover design by Gerald Lee Monks
Cover design resources from dreamstime.com
Inside design by Aaron Troia

The author assumes full responsibility for the accuracy of all facts and quotations as cited in this book.

Additional copies of this book are available by calling toll-free 1-800-765-6955 or by visiting http://www.adventistbookcenter.com.

Library of Congress Cataloging-in-Publication Data:

Nixon, John S., 1954-
Redemption in Genesis : the crossroads of faith and reason / John S. Nixon.
     p. cm.
Includes bibliographical references.
ISBN 13: 978-0-8163-2505-4 (pbk.)
ISBN 10: 0-8163-2505-7 (pbk.)
  1. Bible. O.T. Genesis I–XXII—Theology. 2. Seventh-day Adventists—Doctrines. I. Title.
BS1235.52.N59 2011
222'.1106—dc23
                                                                                    2011040551

11 12 13 14 15 • 5 4 3 2 1

DEDICATION

To Januwoina my love, so faithful

CONTENTS

PREFACE

On the road to Emmaus, Jesus talked with two of His disciples about things He would explain more fully when He spoke to all of them. His talk with those two was the first Christian Bible study. What He said cast new light on the events of the weekend that had been so discouraging to His followers. Jesus explained that His suffering and death were not failures of God's will, but fulfillments of Bible prophecy. "Did not the Christ have to suffer these things and then enter his glory?" (Luke 24:26). Luke records, in words that create in every believer a hunger for a deeper knowledge of truth, what happened next: "And beginning at Moses and all the prophets, he expounded unto them in all the scriptures the things concerning himself" (verse 27, KJV).

With these words, Jesus revealed a new method of interpreting Scripture; a method based on the heart of the gospel—His life, death, and resurrection. With Christ as the interpretive key, Bible students could unlock passages of Scripture* and find in them meaning they couldn't have seen before His coming. The apostles used this hermeneutic in their writings—as illustrated in this passage in which the apostle Paul admonishes God's people to persevere in the faith:

---

* The Old Testament then—it was the only Bible they had at that time—but the whole Bible now.

I don't want you to forget, dear brothers and sisters, about our ancestors in the wilderness long ago. All of them were guided by a cloud that moved ahead of them, and all of them walked through the sea on dry ground. In the cloud and in the sea, all of them were baptized as followers of Moses. All of them ate the same spiritual food, and all of them drank the same spiritual water. For they drank from the spiritual rock that traveled with them, and *that rock was Christ* (1 Corinthians 10:1–4, NLT; emphasis added).

According to Christ, the "new" meaning provided by this kind of reinterpretation of the Old Testament wasn't really new. The shadows and symbols present in the Old Testament were fully unfolded in the kingdom of God that Christ came to proclaim. The Old Testament prophets who were looking for the Messiah exemplified the attributes of Christ in ways even they didn't fully understand. Through them we see how it is that Jesus of Nazareth fulfilled all righteousness by exhibiting all the graces of God in every stage of His life. He is the ultimate meaning of Eden's lamb, of Noah's ark, of Sodom's destruction, of Abraham's ram in the thicket and more.

However, we must realize that our search for the glory of Christ anywhere in Scripture always comes at a price. In the light of His self-revelation, to know Jesus better is to know ourselves better. When we see Him clearly, we see ourselves with increasing clarity, and we suffer by comparison. We discover our beauty is vain, our strengths are weaknesses, and our self-confidence is unwarranted. The revelation of Christ casts our cultural values and our self-esteem into judgment and forces us to choose between His beauty and our self-image. We see the tension between Christ-awareness and self-awareness in the many challenges our Lord presented to His followers as He chastened them again and again for their spiritual blindness, their stubbornness, and their undue pride.

Through this book, I mean to present those same challenges to believers today, calling into question the predominant values of the culture in which we live—a culture that, in the context of the end time, we must scrutinize more thoroughly. In a world where the prophecies of the last days are fast fulfilling year by year, Christ calls His church to a high state of vigilance lest it be taken unawares and fall prey to the enemy's final, overmastering deception that, if it were possible, would deceive the very elect (Matthew 24:24).

In the pages that follow, we will look for Jesus in the stories told in the first book of the Bible, beginning in places where His presence is hidden. We will search out hints of Him and His attributes in shadows and symbols, in metaphors and figures of speech, and, most of all, in the lives of the men and women of yore—believers in the true God, who walked and talked and lived and died in the days before the Messiah came to earth. Through the clarifying lens of Christ, we will see redemption anew as that which calls us to self-abandonment and deeper reliance on Him. We will view redemption from back to front as well as from front to back; from last to first as well as from first to last.

It is my hope that this book will help you to develop an eye more practiced at seeing Christ where He is not overtly shown but where His presence resides nonetheless. Our experience with Him will be all the sweeter for having searched Him out and brought Him forth from the murky shadows and cryptic symbols of Genesis into the clear and glorious light of revelation.

John S. Nixon
November 2011

FAITHFUL REASONING

INTRODUCTION

I call the method of interpreting Scripture that I use in this book "faithful reasoning." I've given it that name because while reason as a way of knowing is essential to our understanding, in the study of the things of God we can rely on it only when it is submitted to the authority of faith, a superior way of knowing. Many writers have made reason the standard by which they evaluate faith, so that reason either validates faith's conclusions or it shows them to be unreliable. However, I assume that reason must be validated by faith rather than the reverse. Since God is the source of all knowledge and faith is essential to pleasing Him (see Hebrews 11:6), even reason suggests that faith must take precedence.

Because it is true that theology transcends the natural realm while secular science limits itself to nature, science can never be the criterion by which faith is judged. Certainly, nature reveals its Creator: the heavens show God's glory, and the world makes His invisible qualities known (Psalm 19:1; Romans 1:20). But since God is not limited to His creation, science and reason cannot disclose all that He wants us to know about Him. That is why in all of the things of God, faith must have priority as "the evidence of things not seen" (Hebrews 11:1, NKJV). Then faith's reasonableness becomes clear—but only to the one who first believes (John 7:17).

As believers, we don't limit ourselves to just two options, as if we

13

have to choose either the rational or the irrational. Rather, we acknowledge the existence of another category peculiar to the spiritual realm, that of the superrational. The existence of a superrational reality means that there are truths that fall into a category that isn't logical but isn't illogical either. There are truths that possess the characteristics of logic—they are sensible, clear, and based on sound reasoning—yet that break through the boundaries of what is quantifiable and explainable. They reach beyond the limits of logic.

The virgin birth of Jesus is an example of the superrational. The biological process of childbirth is clear; it occurs the same way in every case. The sperm and egg unite to form the zygote. The zygote divides and becomes an embryo. The embryo implants in the uterine wall and begins to develop organs—brain, heart, spinal cord, and so on. There are scientifically measurable effects, observable occurrences, and countable stages. The process is logical. But when Mary asked the angel how she would become pregnant since she had never been with a man, the angel didn't give her a biological explanation. Instead, he said, "The Holy Spirit will come upon you, and the power of the Most High will overshadow you. So the holy one to be born will be called the Son of God" (Luke 1:35). When we read the Bible's story, we know we are dealing with something outside of normal biology and beyond the limits of logic. It is inexplicable to our science, but it did take place. Therefore, it isn't irrational.

It is in this realm of the superrational that we find the knowledge of the infinite God. It is reasonable, but it isn't limited to human reason. And in the exploration of what God reveals concerning Himself in Scripture as well as in nature, the disciplines of faith and reason harmonize into a coherent oneness that glorifies God, who is Creator of both.*

THE DOMINANT INFLUENCE

During the period in which modern European philosophy was born, what now is called the Enlightenment, Western culture changed

---

* Alister E. McGrath references the expression coined by Anselm of Canterbury that states the priority of faith over reason, "faith seeking understanding." McGrath adds that while faith comes before understanding, the content of faith is nevertheless rational. See *Christian Theology: An Introduction,* 3rd ed. (Oxford: Blackwell Publishing, 2001), 50.

significantly. The scientific discoveries made during the eighteenth century and the consequent advances in technology convinced many that science was the key to all knowledge. Science and the scientific method became the dominant influence on Western civilization, surpassing the influence of religion and the church. Because the influential members of society now preferred truth that was rational, demonstrable, and accessible to all, divine revelation was discounted as a source of truth. As a result, the term *fact* was used only regarding matters that could be demonstrated scientifically, and the teachings of religion were categorized as mere beliefs. This period saw the triumph of critical rationality at the expense of religious dogmatism.

The thinking of that time brought a new epistemology into being, one that considered any proposition not based on empirical evidence to be inferior. Many people came to regard science as the standard of truth and reason as the light of the world. That period saw the birth of the belief that human progress was inevitable, and people concluded that given enough time, humanity would solve all its problems through the application of rational thought and the methods of science. Ever since then, at least in the West, people have assumed that faith and reason are incompatible and belong to different realms of knowledge. They acknowledge religion to belong to the domain of faith, and consign the material world entirely to the province of reason. Theology was the method of the former, and science the method of the latter, and the proponents of one way of thinking tended to doubt the legitimacy of the other—if they didn't dismiss it altogether.

In this book, I challenge that approach, arguing that not only are the two ways of knowing compatible, they are in fact indispensable to each other. The God who said through Isaiah, "Come now, let us reason together" (Isaiah 1:18), is the same Divine Person who said through the writer of Hebrews, "Without faith it is impossible to please God" (Hebrews 11:6).

Faith and reason are interrelated and interdependent, and they cooperate in the search for truth. Theologians don't attempt to negate rationality or the validity of science and the scientific method. Empiricism has a good track record, yielding positive results in many fields of endeavor: the advances in medicine and technology being prominent examples. But the study of God, His nature and His acts, clearly shows that human analysis alone cannot discover all relevant truths. The power of reason can never discover ultimate truth. The world doesn't explain how it came to be; only the Creator Himself can tell us who we are and why we're here, and this He does through revelation, not through empiricism.

We must remember that we reason in a fallen world, with minds that are finite and subject to sin. The only completely trustworthy science we have is the science of salvation as revealed in the Word of God. Reason alone cannot answer the questions of life because something unreasonable has come in and infected everything.

"We look at life through the eyes of reason and say that if a person will control his instincts and educate himself, he can produce a life that will slowly evolve into the life of God. But as we continue on through life, we find the presence of something which we have not yet taken into account, namely sin. . . . Sin has made the foundation of our thinking unpredictable, uncontrollable, and irrational."[1]

Think for a moment about how completely ludicrous the experience of Job was—how far from reasonable. How could a man lose everything he had in one day? Think of the absurdity of how it all came about—his oxen were stolen, his sheep incinerated, his camels carried off, his children crushed, and other than the four who survived to bring their master the disastrous news, all his servants died as well! Had Job relied on his faculties of reason to deal with what had become of his life, he would have taken his wife's advice, which, under the circumstances, made sense. "Clearly," she said, "God has abandoned you and you are doomed, so be done with it: curse Him now and die!"

The questioning of Job's integrity by his three friends was also reasonable. If God is just and loving and powerful and all-wise, then Job must have done something awful to have deserved what he was suffering. Yet Job's friends were all mistaken—every one of them. There were factors that reason couldn't account for; things the human eye couldn't see. God was up to something that neither Job, his wife, nor his friends could perceive. There were greater issues at stake than any of them could have imagined.

But Job was a faith giant. He didn't need to know all that was going on in order to maintain his integrity. He trusted God even regarding those things he couldn't explain—not because they made sense to him, but because he knew that God was bigger than he could comprehend, and that was all he needed to know. Notice his final confession:

> "Surely I spoke of things I did not understand,
>> things too wonderful for me to know. . . .
> My ears had heard of you
>> but now my eyes have seen you.
> Therefore I despise myself
>> and repent in dust and ashes" (Job 42:3, 5).

In the story of Job, we see how crisis reveals the ascendancy of faith over reason, how it stretches reason beyond the limits of finite human understanding. Reason may be arrogant and sure of itself. Faith is always humble, teachable, and ready to admit that some things happen only by the providence of God.

VIEWS OF THE BIBLICAL RECORD

A critical issue in all of this is how one views the biblical record. Is it just another ancient document to be studied scientifically, or is it the unique expression of the thoughts of God, written down by human writers who were inspired by the Holy Spirit? If the former is true, then faith must be governed by reason. If the latter is true, then it is essential to our understanding that reason be subordinate to divine revelation.

Christian faith has its own method, which by Western standards can only be called unscientific. It isn't objective or limited to the material world and the laboratory. It says that, ultimately, knowing God is a matter of belief—either we choose to trust God and take Him at His word as the Spirit makes it plain to us, or we choose to rely on a system that we control, in which we attempt to verify truth by our own processes.

In writing this book, I have attempted to follow four basic guidelines. Faithful reasoning requires that we

1. *humbly acknowledge the limits of human reason.* Our application of the laws of logic won't necessarily enable us to answer every question we face (Job 11:7, 8).
2. *maintain consistent faithfulness to God.* The One who calls us

to reason is ever beyond the limits of our thinking (Isaiah 40:13, 14). However, He reveals Himself to those who have committed themselves to Him.

3. *offer complete obedience to God.* The only reasonable response of a creature to its Creator is total compliance (Matthew 28:20). God reveals Himself to those who have committed themselves to obey Him.

4. *give priority to faith.* Faith can work where rational explanations flounder (Hebrews 11:13).

If we're honest and courageous, we'll admit that we must give up any idea of discovering truth by our own devices. We'll see that limiting ourselves to a rationalistic approach—relying solely on logical deduction and the laws of cause and effect—is too restrictive. That approach cannot provide answers to the ultimate questions. If we will put our faith in God to the point of a vulnerability that allows us to accept our own limitations, we'll find wisdom and understanding in a new experience of self-abandonment and total dependence on the illumination of the Holy Spirit. "When we are intimately connected with God, He guides our common sense so that faith directs our reasoning instead of logic, which is limited and unreliable."[2]

There is another order of knowledge—one not based on rationalism or the empirical method—that opens the door to eternal truth. It comes to us not by an act of intellect, but by an act of God. Its entryway is repentance and humility before the All-knowing One who condescends to anoint us with wisdom when we come to Him in simple faith. The door to this knowledge is open.

I wrote this book to encourage those who are striving to live their lives by faith as they learn better, day by day, what it means to walk after the Spirit and not after the flesh. It is my intent to help believers who are trying to make decisions that honor God and improve their lives, even if those decisions at times seem unreasonable. Whether or not I reach this worthwhile and lofty goal in the pages that follow, the reader must decide.

May God's Spirit "open the eyes of our hearts" as we seek to know all that Heaven would reveal through the Written Word, always pointing to the Word made flesh.

CHRIST AND CREATION
CHAPTER 1

And God said, "Let there be light," and there was light.
—Genesis 1:3

As soon as we begin to read the biblical account of Creation, we know that we aren't reading science—not our science anyway. The first act of Creation immediately challenges us to make decisions about faith, about what we will choose as the foundational principle of our personal belief systems.

The fundamental axiom of reason in Greek philosophy—"out of nothing, nothing comes"—led to the conclusion that since there was an ordered universe, matter must always have existed. Matter is eternal, and the universe consists of *cosmos* constructed out of *chaos*—form imposed on matter. In other words, God was less a Creator than an Architect who gave form to what already existed.[1]

This principle, now foundational to Western thought, directly contradicts the opening declaration of Scripture, "God spoke and it was done." Only one of these propositions can be true: either matter is eternal or God made all things out of nothing. And logic alone can't determine which one is correct. The acceptance of this fact—that human reasoning can't discover the truth on its own—is essential to settling the question of origins. According to Scripture, the truth of Creation is not based on scientific proof at all. The letter to the Hebrews states the central issue in these words: "*By faith* we understand that the universe was formed at God's command" (Hebrews 11:3; emphasis added).

Science is a reliable guide for understanding things as they are, but it can't tell us why things are as they are.[2] Neither secular science nor Christian theology can tell what happened on this planet before humans existed. Both disciplines build their cases on unproven assumptions. Scientists, beginning with what already exists, reason from effect to cause, believing that careful analysis and logical deduction always lead to the truth eventually. Christians put faith in the Word of God to bridge the gaps that human reason alone can't span, trusting that they can accept its assertions as truth though they will never be able to prove them scientifically.

The most critical issue in the question of origins is the beginning of humankind, the creatures who hold dominion over the earth. Either human beings came into existence randomly and developed gradually through many stages of evolution or they were created purposefully and made complete in the image of God. I take the position that in the natural world governed by cause and effect, if the effect is the material universe, the cause is not eternal matter or preformed microscopic entities. The cause is God. No matter who or how many debate it, Genesis' depiction of the origin of humankind is true: "The LORD God formed man of the dust of the ground, and breathed into his nostrils the breath of life; and man became a living soul" (Genesis 2:7, KJV).

CREATION AND SCIENCE

"The Evolution Wars," an article published in the August 10, 2005, issue of *Time* magazine, documented some of the public debate regarding what should be taught in the classrooms of public schools concerning origins. It quoted then president George W. Bush as saying he believed teachers should present intelligent design alongside evolution so students would know both sides of the issue.[3]

The response of the scientific community, swift and decided, ranged from merely disturbed to completely outraged. Said Mike Padilla, president of the National Science Teachers Association: " 'It is simply not fair to present pseudoscience to students in the science classroom. . . . Nonscientific viewpoints have little value in increasing students' knowledge of the natural world.' "[4] An opinion piece published in the *Winston-Salem Journal* said, "There is a fundamental difference between the theories of evolution and intelligent design. Evolution is science; its tenets have been hammered out over one hundred fifty years through the scientific process of observation and experimentation. Intelligent design is theology. It is not science."[5] Even President Bush's own science advisor, John Marburger, disagreed with his boss, saying, " 'Evolution is the cornerstone of modern biology,' " and " 'intelligent design is not a scientific concept.' "[6] But the editors of *Science-Week* stated their opposition in the most volatile terms of all. They called creationism blasphemy and accused creationists of being primitive thinkers who "believe the Earth is as flat as a pancake, a few thousand years old, and resting on the backs of four giant elephants."[7]

Underlying Marburger's objections was a theme that appeared again and again in the opposition to teaching intelligent design in the classroom: any explanation of origins that isn't "scientific" is, for that reason alone, disqualified. The logic behind the arguments as well as the spirit in which they were given, reflects the values of a culture that has become scientized in almost every field of endeavor, including theology. Now, in order to be considered factual, a proposition must be scientifically verifiable.

Civil libertarians would no doubt have raised the issue of the separation of church and state, but that was not the concern of the scientific community. Their objections to President Bush's statement were based solely on the idea that creationism is religion and not science, as though the two had nothing to do with each other, or at least that one could be complete without the other. In his book *Reason in the Balance,* Phillip E. Johnson describes this cultural bias: "Science is by far our most reliable source of knowledge, [so, in our culture] whatever conflicts with scientific knowledge is [considered] effectively false, and whatever is in principle closed to scientific investigation is effectively unreal. We might say that any supernatural reality or nonscientific knowledge is 'immaterial,' meaning both that it is not based on matter and that it is of no concern to us."[8]

If the human mind is capable of both confession and rationality, it is reasonable to think that there must be a basic coherence between what is believable and what is logical, though we may not always be able to see it. I suggest that there is a way for theology and science to work together harmoniously, but only if theology takes the lead.

Faith, which is an indispensable tool of finite beings, is the foundation of both Christian theology and secular science. Because of our creaturely limitations, in both the material and the spiritual realms, we must rely on the constancy and dependability of things we can't control. Everything in the world of matter depends on gravity, and everything in the realm of faith depends on grace. But as long as science limits itself to the realm of matter and doesn't admit the existence of a spiritual realm, faith and reason will move in different directions; and believers will have to decide which to follow. When the two don't agree, each person must determine which way of knowing he or she will allow to have the ascendancy and which they will permit to languish so the other may flourish.

It is important, even mandatory, for intelligent creatures of an Intelligent Creator to have an intelligent understanding of that Creator and of His works. The Word of God doesn't present its truths in an unreasoned manner, but it does assert truths that extend beyond human powers of reason. The universe we experience through our limited perception has a fullness that only God knows. This suggests a priority of faith over reason since our only access to the truth that is beyond our reach is through belief in the One who alone is able to reveal the unknown.

The Genesis record is the foundation of cosmology, the starting point from which we begin our investigation. In Scripture, there's no mystery to the origin of life. That Divine Book unambiguously declares life to be the work of the Master Designer. It proclaims from the start the absolute sovereignty of the Creator God as the only Maker of heaven and earth. Creation is the sovereign act of God *ex nihilo,* "out of nothing."

But to say that Creation is beyond the scope of science is not to say that the Creation story is itself irrational. The human mind has been ordered by God in accordance with the order of the universe. Therefore, the way in which the world came to be is reasonable, but as one writer put it, "only to that reason which is open to truth that is beyond reason."[9] In other words, when freed from the limited assumptions of human science and placed under the tutelage of faith, we possess the capacity to see the reasonableness of creation "out of nothing." The Creation story is rational, but when the question of origins is limited to the scope of human reason alone, it seems irrational. In that case, the creating of all the various life-forms is misconstrued as an automatic process apart from a Creator, and God is considered to be a bystander in His own universe—a notion that is itself irrational. At times the results of our scientific experiments appear to contradict Scripture's teaching of creation out of nothing. But that doesn't prove that the biblical account is wrong; it only shows that the truth doesn't always conform to our limited understanding.

SOME IMPORTANT QUESTIONS

The suggestion that life has evolved on its own to produce the complicated creatures we see—and are—raises some important questions: How does the concept of a spontaneous creation reflect on the Creator? If the world came into existence by accident and without purpose, what relationship should—or even can—God have with human beings? Is there any room for a sovereign God?

It is legitimate to evaluate a system of belief by the moral framework that comes with it, or, more to the point, by its relationship to God. What good is any belief system that doesn't lead to the true God? This was the substance of Paul's indictment of Greek wisdom (Acts 17:16–23). Christians, including Christian scientists, must never overlook what Darwinian theory does to Jesus Christ. Darwinists must ask themselves whether Christ is still the Living Word who was with God and was God from the beginning (John 1:1, 2). They must ask themselves if He still is the One by whom and for whom all things were created, and in whom all things hold together (Colossians 1:16, 17). If God didn't originate the universe or bring to completion the work He started, then what kind of God is He? Is He really God at all?

The implications of this question extend beyond cosmology. If the origin of human life was totally impersonal, if God wasn't involved, then there is no objective morality, no standard by which all people in every age can be judged. There is only a morality built upon unstable human authority, which may change from culture to culture and era to era and even from person to person. Scripture points to Creation as the sign of God's authority—as what sets Him apart from all other beings as the One to be worshiped and obeyed. His sovereign rule, His immutability and eternity, His wisdom, love, knowledge, and understanding distinguish Him as the One who is above all (Psalms 74:13–17; 102:25–27; 136:5–9). It's because God created the material universe and the creatures that inhabit it that He is worthy of worship and obedience (Revelation 14:7), and no science must be permitted to rob Him of His glory.

All of this is not to deny the important contributions science makes when it is in its proper sphere. Creationism doesn't mean that science must be dislodged from its place in the material world. On the contrary, science is indispensable to human comprehension and control of planet Earth. As Ellen White observed, "God has permitted a flood of light to be poured upon the world in the discoveries in science."[10]

Science is a light in which all humanity has been privileged to walk as we advance farther and farther along the path of understanding the world over which God has given us dominion. But science didn't bring itself into existence. It, too, is a creation. "And it is a confusion of order to make the original derivative and the derivative original."[11] We have exaggerated the authority of science by treating empiricism as though it had no limits, as though it were the only reliable way of knowing. Our worship of the scientific method with its observing, analyzing, experimenting, speculating, and calculating, has inclined us to accept scientific conclusions as undeniable facts even when they directly contradict the Word of God. To quote a plaque said to have hung on the wall of Albert Einstein's office at Princeton University, "Not everything that counts can be counted, and not everything that can be counted counts."[12]

One author has labeled our scientific assumptions a reflection of our intellectual pride and excessive ambition. "In our arrogance we spurn the knowledge that there is any reality we cannot see in a telescope or microscope, or any truth that cannot be reduced to a rational system."[13] Intellectualism often brings with it an air of aloofness, a sense of superiority, and a contempt for simple things. In the early days of the Sophists, the withering effect of intellectualism on the social structure became a cause for concern. It is said that the old men mourned the passing of domestic simplicity and fidelity and the substitution instead of the pursuit of pleasure and wealth unchecked by religious restraint. Historian Will Durant wrote that it "did not make men modest, as it should, but disposed every man to consider himself the measure of all things. Every clever youth could now feel himself fit to sit in judgment upon the moral code of his people, reject it if he could not understand and approve it, and then be free to rationalize his desire as the virtue of an emancipated soul."[14] The scientific method flatters us by accommodating our inclinations to trust in the authority of our own opinions.

Science is one of the tools through which we exercise our God-given dominion, but we must remember that it is the Lord God who was the Creator; in bringing the universe into existence, He was sovereign and acted alone. The dominion of humankind over the earth is a gift, not an achievement. It implies stewardship, not ownership (Genesis 1:28–30). God hasn't given us every power that exists, nor has He revealed to us everything there is to know. God has reserved some things to Himself so that we might in humility remember our place as His children in a relationship based on faith. Ellen White has pointed out the peril of forgetting this truth, reminding us that there are things at stake in the quest for knowledge that have consequences beyond the natural world.

> One of the greatest evils that attends the quest for knowledge, the investigations of science, is the disposition to exalt human reasoning above its true value and its proper sphere. Many attempt to judge of the Creator and His works by their own imperfect knowledge of science. They endeavor to determine the nature and attributes and prerogatives of God, and indulge in speculative theories concerning the Infinite One. Those who engage in this line of study are treading upon forbidden ground. Their research will yield no valuable results and can be pursued only at the peril of the soul.[15]

God didn't begin to build and then leave His work unfinished, like the man of Luke 14:30, who didn't study his project carefully enough before he started it. God no more left Creation to be completed by natural causes than He left Redemption to be completed by human works. When the atonement was completed at the cross, Jesus cried, "It is finished!" and when Creation was concluded on the sixth day, God said "it was very good" (John 19:30; Genesis 1:31).

In the final analysis, the truth of Creation is not a postulate but a principle. It is not a theory but a conviction. It is not a deduction but a confession. It is not by reason but by revelation that we come to know what the Bible never attempts to prove—that the world was created in six literal days of evenings and mornings and that in creating it, God wasn't dependent on preexisting matter. It is "by faith we understand that the universe was formed at God's command, so that what is seen was not made out of what was visible" (Hebrews 11:3). From creeping things to human beings, from earth to sky, from the highest mountain to the lowest valley, and from sea to shining sea, this is our Father's world!

GRACE: ADAM AND EVE
CHAPTER 2

So God created man in his own image.
—Genesis 1:27

The earth and everything in it came forth beautiful from the hand of God. As heads of the human family, Adam and Eve assumed their places side by side over all that God had created for their enjoyment. In the world God had made and in their Eden home, the happy pair had beauty, sustenance, fellowship, and meaningful occupation. They associated with holy angels and with the Creator Himself, and through these associations brought earth into oneness with heaven, a united family with no veil of separation. The man and woman were made vice-regents under God and were responsible to Him.

But the most distinctive and unique attribute that was theirs is expressed in the term *image of God*. This was the ontological description of humankind that linked not just earth and heaven but human nature and divine nature; a term of being that points upward to God, not downward to the animal kingdom. No higher honor could be bestowed upon any creature than to be made in God's image. And though it is beyond our capacities to understand just what it means to be in the image of God—especially now that humankind has been deeply marred by sin—we still can see traces of the image of God in our humanity.* Both comparison with the Holy One and contrast with the animals

---

* Some theologians distinguish between the image of God, which humanity retained after sin, and the likeness of God, which was lost.

reveal the distinctiveness of what it means to be human.

Some of God's attributes are unique to divinity; no created being can possess them. For instance, immutability and infinity in both space and time are His alone; no other beings—not even holy angels—possess these qualities. But there are also divine characteristics that it pleased God to share with His new creation—among them, rationality, morality, and spirituality. In these, we see humanity's intimate connection to the Creator.*

When the patristic fathers considered what it meant to be made in the image of God, they thought of human reason.† They understood the "image of God" to be humankind's rational faculty, which they believed mirrored God's. They argued that this was the endowment that most distinguished human beings from the animal kingdom.[1] It is our ability to reason that enables us to understand the natural realm and detect in it the imprint of nature's God (Romans 1:20). This faculty includes the ability to recognize and organize, to understand and categorize, and to think things through from cause to effect. The power of reason helps us to identify and process the information we constantly receive through our senses. Human reason also includes the ability to think about the future, the ability to draw logical inferences from data and to reach valid conclusions, and the ability to learn from experience so as to adapt and improve.[2] As an example, beavers and human beings both build dams, and when their dams are washed away, both of them rebuild. The beaver builds by instinct, so when it replaces a washed-out dam, it builds something similar to the first one, in the same place, and using the same process and materials. But humans can detect weaknesses and imagine threats, so when they rebuild, they can change the site, improve the design, use better materials, and build a stronger dam, one better able to withstand whatever the future holds.

The power of reason also includes the ability to think transcendently, beyond the limits of human finitude—something we call

---

* Theologians label these endowments *intransitive* and *transitive* or *incommunicable* and *communicable*.

† The leaders of the Christian church in the period following the apostles are called the patristic fathers. Also called the church fathers, they were said to have had immediate contact with the apostles.

imagination. This ability enables us to discover and to engage in reflection, including reflection on ourselves. We can step outside of ourselves and analyze and judge our own actions and even our own thoughts. We can think of ourselves—and even think of ourselves thinking of ourselves!

The image of God also means morality. As beings made in the image of God, we are endowed with an innate sense of right and wrong, the intrinsic understanding that we ought to do some things and that we ought not to do some other things. We can evaluate ideas and actions as matters of conscience. God uses this ethical standard as a mechanism through which to influence us toward the good, which makes the conscience a sacred endowment. As long as we are mentally and emotionally healthy, this faculty sticks with us, commending us when we follow its guidance and haunting us when we violate it.

Conscience is the discriminating capacity to which Paul referred in his letter to the Romans as he wrote about the meaning of our responsibility to God. He described innate morality as the universal standard by which all humanity will be judged, regardless of whether or not they've been directly exposed to God's law. Paul wrote, "When Gentiles, who do not have the law, do by nature things required by the law, they are a law for themselves, even though they do not have the law, since they show that the requirements of the law are written on their hearts, their consciences also bearing witness, and their thoughts now accusing, now even defending them" (Romans 2:14, 15).

OUR INNATE SENSE OF RIGHT AND WRONG

The law of God as expressed in Scripture commands that we love our neighbor as ourselves. And some form of its command that we "do to others what you would have them do to you" appears in almost every religion in the world, even those that are not based on the Bible (Matthew 7:12). There seems to be an innate sense that we are responsible for the way we relate to each other, whether with disregard and harm or in respect and love. This is evidence that we have an innate sense of right and wrong. It is because of this faculty that God is just in expressing His disapproval of us when we violate our consciences, our "law for ourselves," and in commending us when we obey our consciences' directives.

The faculty of spirituality refers to the innate capacity we have to be aware of God as the higher Being outside of ourselves to whom we must give account. It is sometimes labeled as "the sense of Deity." By our very nature, we know that God exists. The spiritual aspect of our nature facilitates our communion with God and enables us to give Him genuine worship. Says the Bible, "God is spirit, and his worshipers must worship in spirit and in truth" (John 4:24). And in Paul's first letter to the Corinthian believers, he asserts that there is an aspect of human awareness other than intellect, and it is from this aspect that the attribute of spirituality springs. He wrote, "Who among men knows the thoughts of a man except the man's spirit within him? In the same way no one knows the thoughts of God except the Spirit of God. . . . The man without the Spirit does not accept the things that come from the Spirit of God, for they are foolishness to him, and he cannot understand them, because they are spiritually discerned" (1 Corinthians 2:11, 14).

So, we can see that as beings made in God's image, we possess not one but two faculties for obtaining knowledge—intellect and intuition. One is rational and the other spiritual. Intellect is the ability to reason, and intuition is the capacity that enables us to commune with God directly, independent of the intellect. As Watchman Nee describes it, the two attributes work together so that we can explain intellectually what we know intuitively. "We do not sense God and the realities of God by our intellect. . . . The mind's role is to explain to our outward man what we know in our spirit and additionally to form it into words for others to understand."[3] We see, then, that intellect is of secondary importance and intuition of primary importance.

Scripture also implies that there is an aspect of spiritual knowing that is beyond the reach of our intellect altogether—knowledge, in fact, that only the Holy Spirit has. Again, the apostle Paul wrote of this: "We do not know what we ought to pray for, but the Spirit himself intercedes for us with groans that words cannot express. And he who searches our hearts knows the mind of the Spirit, because the Spirit intercedes for the saints in accordance with God's will" (Romans 8:26, 27). Nee interprets this biblical principle this way: "Only spiritual understanding can penetrate the spiritual realm. The natural kind may grasp some teachings but these stay in the mind and are unable to flow as life. Because spiritual understanding comes from the spirit it can transform what is understood into life."[4]

Through the ministry of the Holy Spirit, this spiritual capacity enables us to commune with God in ways that our intellectual faculties alone can't. These avenues of communing with God include the spiritual disciplines of meditation and prayer.

There's another factor crucial to our obtaining spiritual knowledge. That factor is belief. The goal of science is to know the things that comprise the material universe—to understand them through objective analysis and to verify our results through repeatable experimentation. But the ultimate goal of theology is to increase our knowledge of God as a Person—to know Him better. Ultimately, theology is subjective, not objective. This becomes clear when we realize that we can't increase our spiritual knowledge without personal commitment. For our minds to be enlightened, we must have a relationship with God, a relationship that is expressed in the obedience of faith. Jesus taught that the perception of truth depends less upon the mind than upon the heart. If truth depended upon reason alone, then pride wouldn't hinder its reception.[5] But as it is, the heart must be emptied of pride and of all unbelief in order to grasp what God wants to reveal through His Son.

Two important verses of Scripture—one from the Old Testament and one from the New Testament, one from David and the other from Christ—describe how this works. Each verse clearly shows that in the wisdom of God, belief comes first and understanding follows.

- "The LORD confides in those who fear him; he makes his covenant known to them" (Psalm 25:14).
- "If anyone chooses to do God's will, he will find out whether my teaching comes from God or whether I speak on my own" (John 7:17).

Here we see that it is a personal relationship rather than objective analysis that enables us to discern the things of God. He causes His sun to shine on the just and the unjust—His self-revelation is universal; but it is our relationship with Him that determines what we are able to understand of that self-revelation (Matthew 5:45). In a psalm recorded in 2 Samuel, David sang,

"To the faithful you [God] show yourself faithful,
   to the blameless you show yourself blameless,
to the pure you show yourself pure,
    but to the crooked you show yourself shrewd" (2 Samuel
     22:26, 27).

And John tells us that when the Father spoke words of affirmation to Jesus shortly before the Crucifixion, some people apparently recognized that what they heard was supernatural in origin, but most people missed it altogether, thinking it was merely thunder (John 12:28, 29).

THE PURPOSE OF OUR EXISTENCE

The attributes of human nature as formed on the model of the divine nature have one goal that overrides every other: to enable men and women, by a free choice based on love, to enter into a personal relationship with God—"to relate to and partake in the life of God."[6] This tells us why we exist. Thus, when God created the Sabbath as a blessed memorial of Creation, it stood as a temple in time in which believers could celebrate the gift of life and the Sovereign Creator who gave it. The Sabbath rest is more than physical rest. Its deeper meaning is the complete reliance on God's finished work that the beings He created revel in on that day, and the gratitude they express to God for being always faithful and steadfast in supplying every need.

Before the entrance of sin, the human family's prospects were full of promise. Grace was in reserve, for it wasn't needed yet; forgiveness hadn't appeared, for there was nothing to forgive. But in order for faith to be confirmed, it must be tested, for this is its nature. Unfortunately, the test didn't go well in its first audition. "When the woman saw that the fruit of the tree was good for food and pleasing to the eye, and also desirable for gaining wisdom, she took some and ate it. She also gave some to her husband, who was with her, and he ate it" (Genesis 3:6).

Eve's downfall didn't begin when she took the forbidden fruit; it began when, rather than trusting God's clear, straightforward command, she started reasoning with the serpent. In the contradiction between the serpent's argument and the command of God, which He gave without explaining (compare Genesis 2:17; 3:4), Eve faced a dilemma, something she hadn't experienced before, and she determined to resolve it herself using her senses and her powers of analysis.

The tree looked as healthy and vibrant as any other tree in the Garden; indeed, it seemed even more desirable than the rest. It showed no signs of decay, and its fruit wasn't rotten nor were its leaves toxic. Eve could see no reason that she should be precluded from eating its fruit. So, for the first time in her existence, Eve doubted God. This was her first step on the path that led to eternal ruin.

Eve didn't think of evaluating her situation subjectively, examining not the tree but the persons from whom the conflicting information had come. She didn't stop to compare the benevolence and love she knew from the Creator, who had provided for her every need, with the inquisitiveness and skepticism she felt when she listened to the serpent, who had given her nothing but a reason to doubt God.

The serpent cast aspersions on God. He suggested that God had a clandestine plan, a secret agenda. He said that God was withholding information it would have been to Eve's benefit to know. Had she taken a minute to consider what this implied about her Creator, she would have reached a better conclusion. Had she compared the persons involved, she would have known which choice was the right one. But Eve thought that cause-to-effect reasoning offered the solution to her dilemma, and her resoning made sense as far as it went. If the tree wasn't harmful, then eating its fruit couldn't result in any harm.

Eve reasoned well, but she didn't reason faithfully. She didn't make personal commitment and loyalty her first considerations. She didn't temper her analysis with love to the One who had given her everything she had, including the power to reason. She placed her faith where it didn't belong—in her own abilities and judgment.

Faithful reasoning always begins with God and His Word and makes God the lens through which we interpret everything else. When we make God anything other than first in our thinking, we have diminished Him, making Him into something less than God. Any reasoning that results in aspersions being cast on the divine character, or that in any way diminishes the divine attributes, can't be sound no matter how unassailable the logic behind it may appear to be. "The fear of the LORD is the beginning of wisdom" (Proverbs 1:7). The scientific method reduces everything to matter, considering even human beings to be little more than the materials that compose their physical being, with no accounting for their spiritual nature. But in Christian theology, the material order is understood through the spiritual reality, the latter being eternal while the former is passing away (2 Corinthians 4:18).

We must remember that the teachings of Jesus are spiritual in nature and that the truth is not a proposition but a Person (John 6:63; 14:6). Therefore, in every endeavor in which we seek to increase our understanding, we need to remember that the "knowledge of the Holy One is understanding" (Proverbs 9:10). When God's command to us is clear, the only rational conclusion is that we must obey it. No amount of analyzing or deducing can lead to an outcome better than the one afforded by simple obedience. And when our Commander doesn't tell us the reason behind the divine command or the reason given seems inadequate, even then obeying Him is the only viable option. God is both the Provider of all we possess and the Judge of all the earth, so, even from a purely self-centered perspective, nothing makes more sense than staying on good terms with Him.

By its nature, sin is mysterious. This is true in part because sin tends to blind the soul. It dulls the moral sensibilities so that sinners don't see their true conditions. Jeremiah's description of the fallen heart's condition seems exaggerated to us. We certainly don't think of ourselves as "deceitful above all things, and desperately wicked" (Jeremiah 17:9, KJV). Rapists, child molesters, serial killers—these are the desperately wicked. Surely, however, that description doesn't apply to law-abiding, tax-paying, churchgoing citizens—the kind of people who would be reading a book like this one. But it does!

THE DAMAGE SIN CAUSES

Because our nature is fallen, it distorts our vision, blinding us to the damage sin causes not only to the sinner but also to others. We say that Adam and Eve were the first to suffer the consequences of sin, and we see how the curse targeted the attributes that were the prime elements of their characters—childbirth becoming painful to Eve, who was to be the mother of the human race, and the earth resisting Adam, the tiller of the soil, requiring him to labor in order to bring forth fruit. But before Adam or Eve felt a single pang, God was already suffering the heartache of the loss of His children's love and loyalty. He was suffering also in anticipation of what sin would cost all those it touched.

Just as parents suffer when their children suffer, so God suffers because of the effect of sin on us, even though we brought it on ourselves. Yet we rarely sympathize with the God who suffers. Indeed, we're more likely to blame Him for the consequences of our sin than to mourn over the heartache our sin has caused Him.

The power of sin runs deeper than it first appears. It doesn't begin with the outward deed or even the conscious thought. Its influence begins at the subconscious level, where ideas germinate and motives are formulated. The sinner is "dragged away and enticed" by evil desire; "then, after desire has conceived, it gives birth to sin" (James 1:4, 15). The moment we decide to rely on our own judgment and take matters into our own hands instead of relying on God and His Word, in that hidden moment, sin makes its appearance. Then we make a choice, and the outward act of disobedience brings to completion the independent spirit that first conceived it.

Sinning is always an act of disobedience to God and His law—"sin is the transgression of the law" (1 John 3:4, KJV). But the essence of sin is the attitude that leads to the act. Whatever the sin may be, its object is always the same: it is God. Sin's first cause lies in the decision—even when it is still subconscious—to turn from total reliance on God to reliance on self. Unbelief and pride are opposite sides of the same coin; the first aimed at God, the second invested in the self. To put it another way, sin is self-worship. It isn't wrongdoing but wrong being. "It is the deliberate attitude that says, 'I am my own god.'"[7] It is the determination to be like God, but not in the way God designed—not by assuming His characteristics through submission. Self-worship means seeking to usurp God's power and prerogatives in universes that sinners create for themselves, ones in which they are (1) omniscient, having the right to know other people's secrets; (2) omnipresent, free to go wherever they please; and (3) omnipotent, with the power to control their own lives and make their own decisions. In the universes we create, we are sovereign, wielding powers like those of the God we have replaced, and Nietzsche's lament becomes ours: "If there were gods, how could I endure not to be a God?"[8]

God has given us free will, but this freedom isn't a blessing in itself. It may be used for good or evil. In fact, because we are born in sin, free will begins as self-will. The miracle of redemption is that, by His grace, God empowers us to use our will for His glory rather than for our own, to choose His loving commands instead of our sinful cravings. In other words, in Christ we have the freedom to give up our freedom in order to follow God's commands with our whole heart. This surrender brings a new freedom—the freedom to do the will of God and, in so doing, find the only freedom that is true and the only peace that lasts.

We find it difficult to believe this principle because it is paradoxical. Jesus highlighted the paradox: "If you cling to your life, you will lose it; but if you give up your life for me, you will find it" (Matthew 10:39, NLT). And when teaching this principle to the Corinthians, Paul wrote of how it worked in his own life: "Though I am free and belong to no man, I make myself a slave to everyone, to win as many as possible" (1 Corinthians 9:19). It isn't self-sufficiency or self-determination that brings joy and fulfillment to the life; it is the unlikely virtue of self-denial that renders obedience to God in everything He commands, even to the smallest detail.[9]

GOD DIDN'T SAY WHY

The test of faith Adam and Eve faced didn't come in what God said; it came in what He left unsaid. He told them what to do—or what not to do—but He never told them why. He established a boundary that they weren't to cross, but He didn't explain why they weren't to cross it.

In God's unexplained command and the serpent's challenge, we see more clearly what was really at stake at the forbidden tree. Eve could take God at His word and obey Him without a reason because she trusted Him, or she could doubt God's veracity and settle the matter for herself. It is a general rule of a relationship that when someone gives a command without giving a reason, that person becomes the reason. The authority of the orders of firefighters to evacuate buildings when there is no sign of smoke depends on the reputation of the firefighters. If they are in uniform and look like firefighters and speak with certainty and a sense of authority, people are likely to regard them as knowing more about fires than they do themselves, and so obey the firefighters. But children in firefighters' uniforms wouldn't garner the same respect. Their commands would make people laugh or annoy the people. The common citizens would be more likely to chastise the children for raising false alarms than to look for any signs of flame.

When a military commander orders his troops to hold a bridge or take a hill at the risk of their lives, the soldiers comply with the orders based on their sense of duty. They've been trained to obey immediately and without question, trusting that their officers know more than they do about the battle plan. When God gives a command without a reason, He stands as the reason—His word being infallible and authoritative. Creatures that exist only because a Creator gave them life have no reason to balk at a command given by that Creator, even if it comes without a reason. The inexplicable is made reasonable by faith. Thus, the arbitrary command—the one that is unexplained—becomes the purest test of a relationship because it rests upon faith in the one who gave the command and upon nothing else.

Eve's real choice was not, Should I or should I not eat? It was, Whom do I believe? Whom do I obey? No doubt because she was deceived she didn't think of it at the time, but her decision was that she wouldn't trust God but rather would take it upon herself to decide her own best interest. Eve took from God the one thing it was most important that she leave in His hands: herself. God entitled humanity to rule the earth and everything in it—the plants and flowers, the birds and beasts, and even the Garden of Eden. But God never gave to human beings the right to rule their own lives, and the forbidden tree stood as a reminder of that fact.

Here we also see more clearly why the Bible introduces the great deceiver by calling him "subtle," or, as rendered by other translators, "crafty," "clever," "shrewd," and "cunning." Satan made the tree the focus of the temptation he brought to Eve, keeping the relational aspect out of sight. Eve contemplated the command, but she didn't think about the Commander. In order to disobey, she had to withdraw her trust in God—which was exactly what the evil one wanted. There was truth in the proposition he made to her, but it was mixed with error. Eve did indeed become like God, but not in the way the serpent suggested—as the enterprising daughter of whom God would be proud. Eve knew good by virtue of being made in God's image, but she came to know evil through rebelling against God; and then, it was an experience that transformed her into the image of the serpent, her new master. By disobeying, Eve changed gods, becoming the unwilling slave of the one she had obeyed. As Paul put it, "When you offer yourselves to someone to obey him as slaves, you are slaves to the one whom you obey—whether you are slaves to sin, which leads to death, or to obedience, which leads to righteousness" (Romans 6:16).

THE FALL

The effect of original sin on Adam and Eve is sobering to contemplate. Because it involves the whole of humanity, we need to be aware of it, and the only way we can fully appreciate the extent of our need for God's grace is to understand the depth of degradation to which we have fallen. Before God confronted the once holy pair or pronounced the curse that sin brought to the earth, changes had already begun to take place in Adam and Eve. These changes were evidenced in the spontaneous actions they took in the aftermath of sin. And "then the eyes of both of them were opened, and they realized they were naked; so they sewed fig leaves together and made coverings for themselves. . . . And they hid from the LORD God among the trees of the garden" (Genesis 3:7, 8).

The instant the parents of our race became sinners, they underwent an internal transformation. They looked the same physically, but their spirits were deeply impacted. Without understanding what had happened to them, they began to act on the basis of the new reality—the reality of sin. Notice what changes sin effected.

- *Honor became shame*—a painful feeling arising from the realization that one is responsible for something dishonorable. When Adam's and Eve's eyes were opened and they knew they were naked, they made coverings for themselves. Never before had their nakedness been a source of concern, but the light of innocence was gone, and they felt exposed.
- *Innocence became guilt*—a feeling that one has done wrong or failed to fulfill an obligation. When Adam and Eve heard the footsteps of God, they hid. Before God spoke to them or asked them any questions, they hid from His presence—something they had never done before. This reveals the deep

pathology of the guilt that was now theirs.

- *Contentment became fear*—a distressing feeling of vulnerability to some impending danger, evil, or pain. Adam explained his hiding: "I heard you in the garden, and I was afraid because I was naked; so I hid" (Genesis 3:10). We think of fear as natural, but it's a consequence of our separation from God. Jesus never felt fear. He was always of good courage when everyone else was afraid. All of our phobias are marks of sin. "God has not given us a spirit of fear" (2 Timothy 1:7, NKJV).
- *Accountability became blame*—attributing fault to someone else. Both Adam and Eve engaged in this false behavior: the exhausting, all-consuming defensiveness in which we rationalize, make excuses, and point the finger at others in a desperate attempt to exonerate ourselves, or, at the very least, lessen our culpability for our own actions.

The noble qualities humankind possessed before sin have all been corrupted. We recognize the traits that replaced them—we've seen them at work in our relationships and life experiences. And now we know where we got them. The shame of sin, the fear of its consequences, and the penchant for blaming others for our mistakes all came to us from our first parents—the apple, as they say, having fallen close to the tree. The pathologies of shame and fear that lead to defensiveness are deeply embedded in our nature. Like our first parents, we engage in the irrational behavior of hiding from God among the trees, as if we could possibly escape His surveillance! We attempt to cover our immoral deeds, not with fig leaves but with finger-pointing and excuses. And every moment of every day we wear masks that we can't remove of our own accord. We wear them out in the world; and when we come to church, we often exchange them for other masks—religious ones—sometimes without even being aware of it.

THE BLAME GAME

In order to understand just how far from God sin has taken us, we need to note how diabolical were the changes that our first parents underwent, and how deeply distorted the image of God they bore became. Comparing the command of God to Adam in Genesis 2:16,

17, with Adam's response to God in Genesis 3:12, enables us to see the devastating impact sin has upon human nature. When God came seeking the man and woman, who had sinned and now were hiding from Him, He called out, "Where are you?" (Genesis 3:9). At that point Adam knew his cover was blown and that he had to face the fact that he'd been attempting to avoid—the fact that he would have to answer to God for what he had done.

God didn't speak of His own aching heart or of the betrayal He felt; His focus was on restoring the broken relationship. So He challenged Adam with a direct and unambiguous question, "Have you eaten from the tree that I commanded you not to eat from?" (verse 11). It's easy to guess what Adam must have thought then. The words God used to confront him brought clear and strong memories of God's warning, and Adam knew that there was death behind the Creator's question. As he remembered that God had said, "*In the day* that you eat of it you shall surely die," he probably thought that the execution of the sentence would immediately follow the verdict (Genesis 2:17, NKJV; emphasis added). This is the context of Adam's response to God; in order to fully understand his response, we must keep this context in mind.

How did Adam respond? He shifted the blame for the capital offense from himself to his wife, saying in effect, "Let the penalty fall on her instead of me. Let her be the one to die." This from the man who had exclaimed when he first saw Eve, "This is now bone of my bones and flesh of my flesh" (verse 23)! This from the man who had named Eve *woman* because she was the counterpart of himself, *man,* and because she had been created from a part of him! Adam had been joined to Eve in marriage; and God, as the officiating Minister, had pronounced them to be one flesh. Eve had completed him. But now, as Adam faced the prospect of certain death, he surrendered his helpmeet to the consequences of the sin in which he had shared, or, as some would say, for which he as the head was ultimately responsible. Indeed, that was God's opinion, as revealed in the fact that He addressed Himself to the man first before confronting the woman.

However, when God did confront Eve, she didn't do much better. She blamed the serpent for her disobedience—as though he had taken the fruit and put it into her mouth. In casting the blame on the creatures God had made, both Adam and Eve were, by implication, blaming Him, their Creator. Their actions confirm the truth that the human heart has become desperately wicked beyond all cure (Psalm 51:5; Jeremiah 17:9; Romans 7:18).

A program on National Public Radio aired the results of a study on the effects of disasters on human relationships—specifically, how man-made disasters differ from natural disasters in their effect upon the mental health of victims. Hurricane Katrina devastated a large part of New Orleans and affected tens of thousands of people, but, by and large, the victims didn't become destructive. Instead, Katrina tended to bring people together. They got involved in the cleanup and recovery efforts, helping each other cope. They joined together in calling upon government officials to provide a quicker and more adequate response. They became more involved in religious activities as the ravages of nature turned their thoughts to their own vulnerability and their need of God. Community was strengthened as people of like suffering bonded.

Human-caused disasters, on the other hand, have a completely different effect on their victims—the 1989 *Exxon Valdez* oil spill and the BP oil spill of 2010 being cogent examples. Neighbors, friends, and family members turned against one another, and domestic violence, divorce, and even suicides increased.

Environmental sociologists and mental health professionals have suggested a reason for the difference. The determining factor was how the sense of brotherhood was affected by the kind of disaster people had suffered. While no one is to blame for natural disasters, in the case of disasters caused by humans, obviously, some people were at fault. But blaming destroys community, and when the sense of community breaks down, people's relationships become corrosive. So there were conflicts over who got contracts for the cleanup work and who received compensation and how much they received for what they had lost.[10]

Like our parents before us, we practice the blame game, too, offering each other up to death so that we can survive. But what we don't always see is that each time we blame someone other than ourselves, we are tacitly blaming God—the One who gave us the husband, wife, child, or parent whom we blame for the sin. We are repeating the original accusations of Lucifer, which are that God is the guilty party, that His laws are unfair, and that free moral agents shouldn't have to be restricted by the laws. We would rather call God a sinner than admit to our own sin—which makes it clear that there's something wrong with us! A plague has become part of human nature, and by virtue of heredity it has been passed to every descendant of Adam and Eve. We see the effect sin has had upon us in what it has done to our spirits. That's the sense in which the penalty of death took immediate effect: Adam and Eve died spiritually on the day they sinned. They became like Satan, thinking like him, and were stirred by his motives, his ambitions, his fears, and his hatreds. And though their bodies lived on for hundreds of years afterward, on the day they sinned, the innate sense of deity that they'd had was snuffed out. Through sin, Adam and Eve lost the unbroken communion with God that had been part of their nature from the moment they were created in His image and likeness. The light of innocence was shattered, and darkness settled upon their spirits.

THE DEPRAVED

In describing the overwhelming effect of sin on human nature, theologians have used the term *morally depraved.* That term speaks of the state of being spiritually dead, a state in which we cannot, in the slightest degree, resist the power of sin. Translated into English, the Latin term for this condition literally means "not able not to sin." In our fallen state, we are helpless victims of sin's power—we can't resist it. Moral depravity means sin works against us from the inside as well as from the outside. It means our natural tendency is to sin even when we're not aware of what we're doing. It's like trying to walk up a down escalator: the momentum is always against us, and it doesn't let up. It frustrates our desires whenever they're turned in any direction other than serving ourselves. We perform some good deed, for instance, something with the potential to bring glory to God, but then we applaud ourselves and feel offended if people don't recognize us for what we've done—especially if they notice someone else's good deed.

Paul described the struggle of every person who has ever felt the longing to be free from sin. He wrote, "I have the desire to do what is good, but I cannot carry it out. For what I do is not the good I want to do; no, the evil I do not want to do—this I keep on doing. Now if

I do what I do not want to do, it is no longer I who do it, but it is sin living in me that does it" (Romans 7:18–20). Paul goes on to cry out in bewildered helplessness, "What a wretched man I am!" (verse 24). This, we realize, is how we feel whenever we are still enough to listen to our inner voices and contemplate our spiritual lives.

Because sin is an attitude and not merely an action, it can express itself not only in immoral behavior but also in behavior that is in itself moral, and there is nothing more dangerous than respectable sin.[11] The teachings of Jesus showed that the strict morality of the Pharisees was based on selfishness rather than on love. They gave generous offerings, but they gave them to be seen. They fasted regularly—but only to impress others with their piety. They said long prayers in public, but they prayed those prayers so their devotion would bring them applause.

The best religious deeds are rendered unacceptable to God and therefore useless when tainted by sin. Sin is first of all a posture of the heart, and it only requires the right circumstances to express itself in outward behavior. Lust is adultery on the way. Covetousness is thievery in embryo. Hatred is murder waiting for an opportunity.[12] And we can no more change these attitudes of our hearts than we can perform heart surgery on ourselves, even if we knew how to do the surgery. Moral depravity doesn't mean that we choose sin; it means that sin chooses us and there is nothing we can do about it. "The carnal mind *is* enmity against God; for it is not subject to the law of God, nor indeed can be" (Romans 8:7, NKJV; emphasis added). This is the condition that became Adam's and Eve's reality the moment they took a bite of the forbidden fruit, and as it was for them, so it is for us; there is nothing in us that can even begin to address our need as fallen creatures. We are totally dependent on unmerited favor for whatever hope we have for the future.

Some years ago a "minor accident" occurred at the Oak Ridge nuclear plant, near Knoxville, Tennessee: one-fiftieth of an ounce of plutonium briefly escaped its canister. The plutonium was returned to the canister within a few seconds, but, by that time, the damage was done. As a result of this tiny, momentary exposure, the entire building in which the accident occurred had to be reroofed and retiled, all of the other buildings within a half-mile radius had to be stripped and repainted, four acres of grass around the building had to be dug up and replaced, one hundred and fifty square yards of concrete had to be torn up and replaced, and twenty-four scientists and technicians needed medical attention—seven of them requiring hospitalization. Sin is like radioactive plutonium—it corrupts everything it touches, damaging many lives, and we can't remove it ourselves.

Some people think they can control the sin in their lives—indulge it when they like and stop whenever they want to. They're deceived. Though with strenuous effort people may overcome negative habits, sin is not so much outward behavior as it is inward corruption. That means that if people eliminate one outward manifestation of the corruption within them, another takes its place. It is impossible for sinners to make themselves good enough to satisfy the claims of God's holy law.

SENT TO CRUSH THE SERPENT'S HEAD

Eve made the wrong choice, Adam joined her in sin, and Genesis 3 catalogs the devastating results suffered by humankind and the rest of the created order—the curse that will last till the end of time. But God had a ready solution—a response to sin that was completely unexpected. Before He told Adam and Eve what sin would do to them, He promised a way of escape, a path to eternal salvation. He said,

> "I will put enmity between you and the woman,
>   and between your offspring and hers;
> he will crush your head,
>   and you will strike his heel" (Genesis 3:15).

Satan didn't fully understand the prophecy, but he knew it was a threat to his kingdom. To bruise a serpent's head is to kill it, so God was prophesying that the reign of sin would eventually end, and He was announcing that the Agent of the devil's demise would be born of the woman. Here was a strategy the enemy never imagined. At the very place where humans were at their worst, God was at His best, revealing a love beyond comprehension. Not even the great intelligence of heaven's brightest angel could have imagined a plan in which God would leave the throne of heaven to join the fallen family of earth, the only fallen family in the entire universe. God gave the promise of this rescue in the very place where the rebellion began, and

He vouchsafed it by a ceremony pointing forward to the One who would purchase deliverance at infinite cost. Genesis 3 opens with the description of the Fall, but it closes with an illustration of redemption. And it is significant that the act of redemption takes place *before* the man and woman are driven from the Garden so they will know that their eviction from Eden doesn't mean they are banished from the presence of God.[13]

Scripture says, "The Lord God made garments of skin for Adam and his wife and clothed them" (verse 21). This wasn't merely the shearing of a live animal to make a coat that would protect them from the cold. Something deeper was revealed here. Because the skin of the creature was to be taken, it had to die. What happened to the sheep exemplified the means by which humanity would be saved from the penalty of sin. Christ would bear the entire cost of redemption. Someone who is justified is declared "not guilty"; but in the redemption God provided, that verdict isn't based on the criminal's righteousness—it is based on the innocence of the Advocate being credited to the criminal, however undeserving he or she is.

Sanctification, which follows justification, means to be made holy. It is the lifelong process by which the criminals grow into the innocence that was conferred in the verdict. Living the life of faith dependent on their Redeemer and His righteousness produces in them His attitude and actions. This, too, is a gift undeserved.

Even though sinners make no contribution to the procuring of their freedom, those who have been set free must pay a price, however. As the father of the human family offered his first sacrifice, he trembled at the sight of the bleeding, writhing animal that wouldn't be suffering were it not for his transgression. It pained him to see what his rebellion had caused, and all the more as he contemplated the day when the Lamb of God would come to take away the sin of the world. This was by far the greatest burden the curse of sin would place on repentant sinners—their realization of the price God must pay, of the pain He must suffer, to effect their salvation. It seemed to Adam that he was shedding the blood of God's Son with his own hand.[14] He was overwhelmed with guilt and humiliation, but he must shed the blood of the Sacrifice.

Here is where so many of us fail. We don't avail ourselves of the full blessings of God's grace because of the painful humiliation that of necessity comes with it. When Adam and Eve sewed fig leaves together to make coverings for themselves, they were doing the best they could to address their situation. It was a perfectly natural reaction. When the consequence of sin comes home to us and we are filled with regret, we want to do something to make things right. We want to do whatever we can to redeem the situation. The knowledge that we have at least done *something* would be a source of some comfort, some satisfaction, some pride. But that would take grace out of the equation. Grace means that we receive something we didn't achieve and don't deserve. It isn't merely something we couldn't accomplish ourselves, but something we couldn't have even thought of on our own. Grace means accepting the power of another in place of our inadequacy. It means relying on something we had no hand in bringing about. Grace is charity, and we may consider receiving it without paying for it to be humiliating, but there is no other way to be saved. Grace is part of a package deal; we must accept the humiliation with the exoneration.

Nobody will strut proudly into the kingdom of God having made it there on their own. All the redeemed must bear the burden of culpability for the death of God's Son, and that destroys all pride. As recipients of salvation that has been given to us freely, we have nothing to boast about. We must surrender any claim to the onlookers' applause. No one who receives grace can boast (see Ephesians 2:9). Those who receive it do so on the basis Paul wrote about to the Corinthians: "What do you have that you did not receive? And if you did receive it, why do you boast as though you did not?" (1 Corinthians 4:7; see also Luke 17:7–10).

The grace of God operates on laws that differ from those of nature. Everything in the world of nature is fixed, predictable. But suddenly, the supernatural—a new life principle—invades the natural world. This is not merely goodness; God's goodness flows throughout the entire unfallen universe. No, this is something different; this is goodness undeserved, favor unwarranted. Grace brings blessing where cursing belongs; it brings forgiveness where there should be condemnation. Humankind's fall into sin meant that if any humans were to be saved, there must be another creation. So, on the day when sin contaminated the earth, God created salvation for the whole human family; not just for Adam and Eve, but also for all those who were yet to be born. And the vehicle by which this salvation commuted from heaven to earth was grace. As Adam and Eve tearfully turned their backs on the tree of life, never to taste of its fruit before their deaths, they wore the clothing God had provided as the symbol of the righteousness of Christ. The promise found in Genesis 3:15 took away the nakedness and shame pictured in Genesis 3:7, 8.

WHEN LIFE WAS LOST

Because of God's grace, the laws of nature were disrupted. The effect that should have followed the cause was diverted, so the sinners didn't die immediately. Instead, the fallen rose again; they found abundant life. The light of creation, brought into existence by the spoken word, had its complement in the light of redemption bought at a great price through the sacrifice of the Living Word. The word spoken originated life, and when life was lost, the Word made flesh restored it. The sacrifice of the animal in order to provide the garments of skin represented the death of Jesus, which was required in order to provide the robes of righteousness believers wear. As soon as there was sin, there was a Savior. Thus we see Jesus, as Redeemer, in Genesis. The goal of redemption has always been that we should have the death-free, incorruptible life of Jesus Christ, but not as our own attainment. It comes only as the gift of grace, which is ours by faith in Christ alone.

His divine name is the Son of God; His celestial name is Michael the Archangel; and His human name is Jesus Christ. The glory of divinity is seen in all three of these revelations, but in none more clearly than in the revelation of God in human flesh. Jesus Christ is the One who abides with us and in us forever by His Spirit when we put our trust in Him. Then we become "more than conquerors through him who loved us" (Romans 8:37). "Christ in you," Paul wrote, is "the hope of glory" (Colossians 1:27). On this subject Ellen White is powerfully eloquent: "Nothing is apparently more helpless, yet really more invincible, than the soul that feels its nothingness and relies wholly on the merits of the Saviour. God would send every angel in heaven to the aid of such a one, rather than allow him to be overcome."[15]

I broke my son's arm when he was nine months old—by accident, of course. Before his birth I had always been slightly nervous holding newborns; I was afraid of their fragility. But after nine months I was comfortable not only holding but also playing with my son—a little too comfortable as it turned out. The mishap occurred when I swung him by his arms. At first there was no sign of it—there hadn't been any popping sound and not a whimper of pain from my boy. He seemed to enjoy the game as much as I did. However, soon after I stopped swinging him, his mother noticed that he wasn't using his right arm. Other than that he played as though nothing was wrong. He didn't perceive his broken condition, but we did.

A call to the pediatrician sent us quickly to his office, and he confirmed our amateur diagnosis—one of the bones in our son's arm had slipped out of place, and he couldn't use that arm. The doctor said he could fix it, but the repair would be painful. Fittingly, I was to be the one who held my son while the doctor snapped the bone back into place. Though I was the guilty party, I was to join in the cure of the one I had hurt. I, who had provided him with provisions and protection, would now be among those who caused him pain.

My son settled into my arms without fear, but I was anxious—we couldn't explain to him what we were about to do to him or why we were going to do it. He was looking to Daddy to protect him, but in order to aid in his cure, Daddy was going to join with those who would hurt him. I was about to betray my son—at least that's what it seemed like to me—but there was no other way to solve the problem.

When the doctor expertly popped the bone back in its place, my son cried out in pain. But then the arm that had become dormant swung back to life—as my boy reached, not for me, but for his mother. When he was in the comfort of her embrace, his tears soon dried. My heart, however, cried on a little longer.

The cost of grace is pain, both to Jesus and to us. But His pain was infinite in comparison with ours. Every disciple of Jesus Christ is called to the life of suffering. Jesus said, "Take up [your] cross and follow me" (Matthew 16:24). The humiliation grace brings to us as humans prone to pride is the entryway into that life. And if the humiliation of being dependent upon undeserved merit seems to be a hard thing to accept, then we should look at the suffering that brought grace into existence on the cross of Jesus Christ. To refuse the gift that He offers freely is to extinguish from our lives all hope of experiencing the redemption bought at so great a price.

Some of the inhabitants of the Pacific Northwest suffer a health

GRACE: ADAM AND EVE

problem that is sometimes blamed on the weather patterns of the region. Its cloudiness causes a condition doctors call seasonal affective disorder, or SAD. Its symptoms include severe mood swings and fits of depression; in the cloudy times of the year, the suicide rate is elevated.

The cause of the sickness is light deprivation. People who suffer from SAD are gloomy because of the lack of sunlight. One of the treatments involves using special light panels in the home to give the victim heavy doses of illumination to counteract the depression and its destructive results. Light is the only cure for the lack of light.

The same holds true in the spiritual realm. Since the entrance of sin into the world, the whole human family has been suffering from SAD under the darkness and gloom of the prince of this world. The only cure is the light that shines from God through His Son, Jesus Christ.

Earlier we spoke of the condition of moral depravity expressed in the Latin as "not able not to sin." As it turns out, by virtue of God's grace the condition has a counterpart in the final state of the redeemed. When the blood of Jesus and the work of His Spirit reach full maturity in their lives, they will become morally pure, not able to sin. Not that God will have taken the power of choice from them, but that through the grace of Christ, their decision to serve God will have become permanent, and choosing not to sin will be as natural to them as choosing to sin used to be. They will have settled into a state of permanent loyalty to God from which they will never turn back.

This is the state of the redeemed when Jesus proclaims, "He that is righteous, let him be righteous still: and he that is holy, let him be holy still" (Revelation 22:11, KJV). It is what Ellen White had in mind when she wrote that the seal of God wasn't a "seal or mark that can be seen, but a settling into the truth, both intellectually and spiritually, so they [the redeemed] cannot be moved."[16] It isn't a matter of human perfection, but one of complete and utter trust in the perfection of Christ. It is the final accomplishment of God's grace in the redeemed.

"Without the grace of Christ, the sinner is in a hopeless condition; nothing can be done for him; but through divine grace, supernatural power is imparted to the man, and works in mind and heart and character. It is through the impartation of the grace of Christ that sin is discerned in its hateful nature, and finally driven from the soul temple."[17]

BROTHERHOOD: CAIN AND ABEL
CHAPTER 3

We know that we have passed form death to life, because we love our brothers.
—1 John 3:14

A s is evident in the text above, Scripture portrays Cain's worship as not only unacceptable but actually offensive to God. The apostle John called it evil. But when we look at the story through twenty-first-century eyes, we wonder why God's response was so harsh. Cain didn't ignore God as if He didn't exist. He was no atheist. In fact, we see only a hard-working laborer presenting to his Lord the best he had—the fruit of the sweat of his brow. What was so wrong about that? Is not worship defined as the act of giving back to God our best as a token of our thankfulness to Him? If anything, we would expect Cain's offering to be more acceptable to God than Abel's was, since Cain gave something he had worked for with his own hands, while Abel presented only something he had cared for, not something he had produced. But as we are soon to see, this is exactly the point of the story—the difference between worship as one's own work and worship as God's finished work.

Biblical interpretation differs from that of most other literature, in that the interpreter must account not only for the particularities of time and place but also for the difference between the human and the Divine. Intellect alone cannot do this. As the only Creator and Redeemer, God is unique (Romans 11:33). Because we are created in His image, our minds can be adapted to God's way of thinking. It is apparent, for example, that the Word of God and the human soul were made for each other.

But this adaptation doesn't happen naturally, as though the capacity were already in us. We are unspiritual (Romans 7:14), so we will never be able to claim an exhaustive knowledge of God. We cannot know God the way He knows us or even the way we know each other. We can *apprehend* but never fully *comprehend* the divine wisdom and majesty. We can grasp divine truth and hold it in our hands, but we can never get our arms all the way around it. We can't answer every question or solve every puzzle concerning God's mysterious deeds in the earth, or even in our own lives. We'll never be able to say that we know God the way we know our child or sibling or spouse because they are like us in nature. Nor will we find that any of the norms of any human cultures will do justice to divinity or to the value system of heaven. Human cultures may have some standards that are consistent with the values of God's kingdom, but none so thoroughly reflects the divine character as to be called holy as God is holy. Like individual human beings, all cultures have sinned and come short of God's glory. In order for us to understand Scripture, the light of the Holy Spirit must illuminate our unholy minds.

The Old Testament passage from which the principle of Romans 3:23 was derived dramatizes in a compelling way the gap between the Holy God and His fallen creatures. It depicts God as looking down from heaven on the whole human family in search of one good heart—just one righteous person who seeks God of his or her own accord. We imagine God's eyes roaming to and fro throughout the planet, searching through every nation, every time zone, and every era of human history, but He can find none who measures up. "There is no one who does good, not even one" (Psalm 14:3). This is the divine assessment of where the world stands in relation to heaven and its values, and we must be humble enough to accept this truth as we seek to understand God's Word. We must place our personal values and standards in submission to the divine value system as revealed in God's dealings with the human family. Therefore, if we want to understand the saga of Cain and Abel correctly, we must, through the illumination of God's Spirit, see it from the Divine viewpoint.

THE NARRATIVE

Abel is lying motionless on the ground. He won't be getting up. His heart has stopped beating. His brain function has ceased. His lungs no longer expand and contract with the breath of God. The new, dark destiny of humanity that arrived with the entrance of sin has struck the first family full bore.

Abel is dead. Beneath him innocent flowers wilt under the weight of newly spilt blood. Above him, his older brother shudders with the burden of fresh guilt. And beyond them both a Holy God grieves to see what has become of His creation.

Though Cain stands over his brother's lifeless body, he does not realize the full significance of what he has done. The great controversy, which began in heaven, has engulfed planet Earth now, too, and Cain has become its first combatant and Abel its first casualty.

The Bible spares us the grim details. It doesn't tell us exactly how Cain accomplishes his dastardly deed, whether with a weapon or with his bare hands, and if with a weapon, whether with a sharp one or a blunt one. We only know that the world's first baby has become the world's first murderer, and neither he nor the world will ever be the same again.

Cain does not know it, but his sin will set off a chain of violence that will spread throughout the earth and into every generation of humankind. From this day forward, Satan will use murder as one of the chief weapons with which he will accomplish the ruin of human souls, souls of both victims and perpetrators. Before he is finished, not only will brothers be killing brothers, but husbands their wives and wives their husbands, parents their children and children their parents; eventually, people will kill strangers and nations will destroy nations in a holocaust of carnage that will last to the end of time.

Under the pristine skies of primitive earth it seems inconceivable, but a day will come when a whole new lexicon will have to be invented just to describe the many strains of murder that curse the human family: *homicide, infanticide, genocide,* and *suicide; annihilation, assassination, massacre,* and *manslaughter; bloodshed, butchery, execution, slaying, felony, liquidation, lynching, offing,* and *snuffing.* This violent vocabulary will make its way into headlines and novels, into dictionaries and encyclopedias, and into movies and video games so that even children will become versed in it. Eventually, murder will become so domesticated as to be fictionalized for entertainment, industrialized as commerce, politicized in ideology, and rationalized through psychology.

The thought never enters the mind of Cain, but a day will come when nations will train their armies in the science of killing other armies; they'll spend a king's ransom on implements of war specially crafted to destroy human beings on land, on sea, and in the air. They will even develop such horrifying sophistication as to be able to push a button and launch death-carrying missiles into the air—missiles that travel great distances and, with pinpoint accuracy, enter through a particular door and detonate against a specific wall, taking out everything within the reach of the blast. And people will celebrate this technology as a great achievement, the way angels celebrate when a soul is born into the kingdom of God, and an act that was alien and horrific in the beginning will become so commonplace as to seem natural to humankind—even to the extent that we could hardly imagine life without it.

And all of this begins with two brothers alone in a field, one of them with hatred in his heart. To understand the biblical significance of the Cain event, we must study not the outward deed that exhibited it, but the inward motive that prompted it, for whatever Cain did to his brother outside the gates of Eden, he did out of the dark corruption of a fallen nature—a nature just like ours. And though we would feel comfortable saying that we have never taken a human life, we are to discover that from Heaven's perspective, we, too, may be guilty of murder.

MEANT FOR REPENTANCE

In the aftermath of Cain's sin, God questioned him as He had Cain's father: "Then the LORD said to Cain, 'Where is your brother Abel?'

" 'I don't know,' he replied. 'Am I my brother's keeper?' " (Genesis 4:9).

In the case of Adam and that of Cain, God was probing the state of the relationship between Himself and them, meaning to arouse conviction that would lead them to repentance. In Adam's case, the question was direct: "Did you disobey Me and eat from the tree I commanded you not to eat from?" (see Genesis 3:11). In the case of Cain, the question was indirect but just as meaningful: "What have you done?" (Genesis 4:10). When God questioned Adam, Adam became evasive. When He questioned Cain, Cain became defiant, responding, in effect, "Why should I care?"

But the men responded differently. When Adam discovered the magnitude of his sin and that it would cost the life of God's Son to save him, he was so filled with grief that he offered to die for his transgression.[1] Cain had no such thought. He short-circuited the entire interrogation process with a question of his own, one with which he meant to justify himself: "Am I my brother's keeper?"

Cain's question, raised defensively, becomes the point of the drama—the reason the story was turned into scripture. Cain's attitude toward Abel's death illustrates by contrast the biblical teaching of brotherhood, the most important command Jesus gave to the end-time church, a command that captures the essence of what it means to be a commandment keeper in the last days: *you are your brother's keeper* (John 13:35; Galatians 5:14).

Sin made its debut in the Garden of Eden. Now it returns for the second act stronger than it was before. Adam committed sin without admission; Cain committed sin without remorse. And once he had spurned the spirit of repentance, he conformed his life to the intransigent attitude that he had adopted. Adam and Eve had bowed under the weight of guilt. Cain, too proud and self-sufficient to bow to anything, wouldn't repent. He warded off any feelings of culpability by denying that his deed was wrong. Defiant, he smothered the voice of conscience until he could no longer hear it.

In response, God did an unusual thing. He put His mark on Cain. Not only did He refrain from directly punishing the murderer, He prevented the natural chain of consequences that punishes sin with sin from taking its usual course. Divine power, which Cain defiantly ignored, was enlisted to protect him from the consequences he deserved (Genesis 4:13–16).[2]

God banished Cain from human society; and in his exile, Cain lived only to banish God from his heart and from his life. Cain married. He had children. He built a city and a civilization. He developed a culture based on sin, one that institutionalized defiance toward God. He instilled in his progeny the same spirit of rebellion he had adopted in his own life, and his wicked influence spread from generation to generation until he became the head of a new line of men, the high-handed sinners of the antediluvian world. This was the fallen generation for whom sin was not a result of weakness or ignorance, but of daring rebellion against God. As would later be said of Ahab, one of Israel's most notorious kings, the antediluvians excelled in doing things to enrage God until the Creator regretted that He had ever made human beings. Eventually, the human race reached its most degraded condition ever, as pictured in the shocking description in Genesis 6:5: "Every inclination of the thoughts of his heart was only evil all the time." Notice the terms: "every," meaning without omission; "only," without variation; and "all," without exception.

THE RESULTS

From the time of Cain onward there were to be two distinct lines of the human family, both descended from Adam. The sons of Seth, Abel's replacement in the patriarchal line (Genesis 4:25),* began to call themselves sons of God. The line of Cain, the rebel against God, called themselves the sons of men.

Cain should have been executed for his crime, but God commuted his sentence. He permitted Cain to live in order to demonstrate to the universe what happens when sin goes unpunished, when wickedness isn't brought to justice, when evil is not followed by swift and decisive judgment. This is the legacy that comes down to us from the primitive earth. This is how the history of humanity began. And since that day, the spirit of Cain has become rife in the world. When Seth's descendants began to intermarry with Cain's descendants, the violence spread until it engulfed all of humanity (Genesis 6:2).

The story of sin and death is not just the story of our rebellion against God, it is also the story of our hatred toward each other—man's inhumanity to man. These two have coexisted from the beginning. The story of the Fall doesn't end in Genesis 3; it continues in

---

* *Seth* means "appointed," as in appointed to replace Abel, or compensation for Abel.

Genesis 4. The path that leads from the Garden of Eden is littered with not only forbidden fruit, discarded fig leaves, and the carcass of a lamb, but also the corpse of a young man who never married and never had children because his life was cut short in hatred and jealousy by his own brother.

It is said that you don't have to put a lid on a barrel of crabs. You won't lose any because as soon as one climbs high enough to be close to escaping, the others pull it back in. People call this phenomenon "crabs in a barrel," but someone has suggested that crabs have a name for this too—they call it "acting like humans." We are the ones who brought sin—with its legacy of brokenness, violence, and bereavement—into the world. Sin is the gloom and darkness that covers the whole earth, affecting every living thing, though its most egregious acts are the ones we commit against one another. God expresses in emphatic terms His loathing of the things we do to hurt each other:

> There are six things the LORD hates,
>   seven that are detestable to Him:
>   haughty eyes,
>   a lying tongue,
>   hands that shed innocent blood,
>   a heart that devises wicked schemes,
>   feet that are quick to rush into evil,
>   a false witness who pours out lies and
>   a man who stirs up dissension among brothers (Proverbs 6:16–19).

The story of Cain is a lesson in tragedy. We learn from him that *people who don't repent go further and further into sin until their hearts become so hard that they no longer can repent.* And not even God can save a soul that has not been yielded to Him.

MURDERERS?

On June 4, 2004, the *San Francisco Chronicle* reported that a full-term baby boy had been found dead in a garbage can. The baby's seventeen-year-old mother had sought medical care for vaginal bleeding. When the hospital personnel found a freshly cut umbilical cord and questioned her, she denied having been pregnant. But the authorities conducted a search and found the dead baby in a garbage can in front of the young woman's home.[3]

In another case, a teenager went to her high school senior prom, gave birth while there, cut the umbilical cord, and choked the infant to death. She then placed the corpse in a plastic bag, disposed of it in the bathroom trashcan, and returned to the dance.[4]

These horrifying stories are instances of what some are calling the growing phenomenon of *neonaticide*—the murder of an infant within the first twenty-four hours of its birth. In these cases as in others, the maternal perpetrators weren't suffering from mental illness or postpartum depression. They were acting out a carefully crafted plan. These young women hid their pregnancies from their families and classmates, confiding only in their closest friends. They gained very little weight. They concealed their morning sickness and wore clothing that disguised their bodily changes. They then secretly gave birth to and killed their newborns before they were discovered, bringing the legacy of Cain to terrifying new heights.

As we read about extreme behaviors like these, we distance ourselves from them, convincing ourselves that they have no relevance to us. It's easy for us to disassociate ourselves from such dastardly deeds. But when the Cain story is taken up in the New Testament, the focus is not on the outward act of murder, but on the underlying motive that prompted it. The apostle John gives us an expanded definition of what it means to be a murderer, widening the circle of those who, in God's sight, are guilty of this heinous crime. He wrote, "Anyone who hates his brother is a murderer, and you know that no murderer has eternal life in him" (1 John 3:15).

This striking and disturbing passage articulates a value system far different from what we are accustomed to. Murder has faces that are more subtle than physical violence. Some of the incarnations of murder may even be outwardly benign—aggressive in a passive way. But though murder cloaks itself in a multitude of disguises, all have the same underlying identity. Thus, when our conversation includes gossip, slander, or backbiting, Scripture may charge us with murder. Under John's definition, irritability, petulance, and exasperation can reveal a bent toward murder. And even apathy may be murder in God's sight when it takes on the heart-hardened posture that says, "Other people's problems are their own concern; I have no responsibility for them." Humans judge by outward appearance; the Lord looks on the heart, and His penetrating eyes see attitudes and actions that reveal us all, like Cain, to be murderers. And in John's epistle, we are being called to repentance.

A minister new to the church he was serving was called to the home of a deacon whose wife had just died. When the deacon began to inquire about making arrangements for a service at the church, the pastor asked whether he really wanted a church funeral for his wife. Surprised, the deacon asked the reason for the pastor's question.

The pastor lowered his voice and said he had heard that the deacon's wife was a backslider who had stopped attending church years earlier. People told him that she stayed home all day, wearing a negligee, and always keeping a glass of liquor within reach. Worst of all, the minister said, he'd been told that once a week while the deacon was at work, a stranger driving a car with out-of-town license plates would enter the house, stay about an hour, and then slip away before the deacon got home.

By the end of the story, the deacon was in tears. "Pastor," he said, "two years ago my wife contracted a terminal disease with no hope of recovery. The disease made her skin so sensitive that she could wear only the lightest clothes. The 'glass of liquor' was her medication, which she had to take every hour. And the stealthy out-of-town visitor was a specialist who came every week to give her a treatment.

"The church members haven't known the truth of the matter," the deacon said, "because no one ever called to see why we'd stopped coming to church."

What the church members said about the deacon's wife added new grief to that which her death had brought. He felt as if he had lost her twice. Long before his wife passed away, the church had murdered her by their evil surmising.

In his first letter, the apostle John said, "This is how we know what love is: Jesus Christ laid down His life for us. And we ought to lay down our lives for our brothers" (1 John 3:16). And in the other John 3:16, we find the call of God to recognize the truth of the life-or-death choice that is set before us as Christians: we can choose murder or self-murder. We can become murderers of our brothers and sisters, or we can choose to sacrifice ourselves for them, to lay down our lives for them. We can be killers, or we can surrender our lives. We can't do both. The choice is just that concrete.

When a noun is a verb

There is something about divine love that we tend to miss at first because of our earthly mind-set. In Scripture, love is always active. Even when it's a noun, its innate meaning always involves an action. Love isn't merely a religious concept or a speculative idea. In the Word of God, there is no "love" in the abstract. Love is as love does. Jesus Christ's command that we love one another is a gospel imperative. It's the litmus test of true conversion: either we love, or we don't belong to Christ. "We know that we have passed from death to life, *because we love our brothers*" (1 John 3:14; emphasis added).

As Christians, we are held to a different standard than other people are. It isn't enough for us to be polite, to live quietly and cooperatively with our neighbors, to pay our bills and our taxes on time, and to mind our own business. Love is not merely harmless—it is assertive and proactive, reaching out in good deeds toward others wherever it finds need. Our Lord said He came into the world to serve, and the apostle Paul called himself a bondservant for Jesus' sake (Luke 4:18; 2 Corinthians 4:5). Because of Christ's love for us and for the glory of His kingdom on this earth, we *are* our brothers' and sisters' keepers. Whatever builds people builds the kingdom of God. We can't inherit eternal life without having the love of God rule in our hearts. Love is as love does. And what does love do? It lays down its life for a brother or sister. This doesn't necessarily mean dying, but it *does* mean sacrificial living, and it has meaning only in action.

Confused ideas of love and compassion abound in our culture; they seem to reside in every quarter of society. There is probably no godly concept that has been more universally distorted than the concept of true love. For thousands of years 1 Corinthians 13, which has come to be known among Christians as the love chapter, has declared the nature of true, godly love in clear, compelling language. Within its thirteen verses are challenging ideas that confront and confound the traditional assumptions regarding what constitutes true religion:

- "If I have a faith that can move mountains, but have not love, I am nothing."
- "If I . . . surrender my body to the flames, but have not love, I gain nothing."
- "Love is patient, love is kind. . . . It is not easily angered, it keeps no record of wrongs."
- "Love never fails."

And then comes the summary statement that clinches the claims of love's supremacy over all other Christian virtues:

- "And now these three remain: faith, hope and love. But the greatest of these is love."

The Corinthians of Paul's time thought spirituality meant special gifts and secret knowledge. They took pride in demonstrations of spirituality such as speaking in tongues, and they vied for acknowledgment as spiritual leaders. Paul wrote to correct this false priority and to direct the focus of the believers back to the one true priority of Christian living: love.*

The church today needs to have the same corrective applied to it. God's people of the last days need spiritual revival, but we don't need to focus on being better tithe-payers, better health reformers, or even better Sabbath keepers in order to achieve it. All of these virtuous acts will not only be sustained but amplified when we pursue the high calling to which Christ beckons us. By the grace of God we need to focus on becoming better lovers as brothers and sisters in Christ. This is John's antidote to the spirit of Cain, and God is longing to give it to us if we are willing to receive it.

The story is told of an attorney who, after meditating on Scripture, decided to cancel the debts of all his clients who had owed him money for more than six months. He wrote a letter explaining his decision and its biblical basis and sent copies of it by certified mail to seventeen

---

* The whole of 1 Corinthians 14 presents Paul's corrective on this matter. Notice also how the closing verses of chapter 12 transition into the love theme of chapter 13.

of his clients. But one by one sixteen of the letters were returned unsigned and undelivered. The clients had refused to sign for the delivery—being in arrears, they feared the attorney was suing them to collect his debts.

How profound! Like that attorney, God is sending out debt-canceling letters to us based on His love. But in order to receive the benefits, we must open our hearts to His love.

LOVE'S SOURCE

"Everyone who loves has been born of God and knows God. Whoever does not love does not know God, because God is love" (1 John 4:7, 8). The love we are called to live by in Christ, the love of 1 Corinthians 13, is not natural affection. The love that comes from God doesn't have its source in human nature; it must come from somewhere else.

We all possess natural affection—the capacity to love others based on affinity. We're just naturally drawn to some people. We want to be around them, do things with and for them, speak to them, and have them speak to us, and this is a good thing as far as it goes. But it is not the love to which Jesus is calling us as brothers and sisters in Him. This kind of love has the mark of death on it because it is destined to perish with this world. It is the love of those who share our tastes and opinions, who think like we do. It is the innate love of friends and family that we recognize even in its absence, that disturbs when it is neglected, and that horrifies us when it is abused. When we say that in order to love others we must first love ourselves, this is the love we are speaking of, whether or not we know it. If we love others based on loving ourselves, we end up loving the reflection of ourselves in others. That is self-centered love, a contradiction in terms.

When we think of the supernatural in Christianity, things such as miracles, healings, and outstanding spiritual gifts come to mind. We think of Jesus healing the man born blind, a miracle of love indeed (John 9). But all of Christianity is supernatural, even those aspects that to us seem mundane. When Jesus commands us to love one another as God loves us, He is speaking of a miracle. These words are not directed to the natural human being at all; Jesus is speaking to the new creature imbued with His Spirit. We are not to look to ourselves for the love of 1 John 4 or 1 Corinthians 13; we won't find it within us.

The only Source of the love to which God calls us is God Himself. God is love. We can receive His love only from Him. We have to pray for it and fast for it and stay connected to Him in order to receive it. When we do by His grace, we are empowered to love people for whom we have no natural affection, who do not look like us or think like us and who may even be our enemies. Love's only true source is God, and Jesus is its ultimate Example.

LOVE'S MOTIVATION

"As I have loved you, so you must love one another. By this all men will know that you are my disciples" (John 13:34, 35). These are the words Christ used to describe the sign of true discipleship. That sign is not Sabbath keeping. The Sabbath is the sign of God's identity in the earth. It stands for His sovereign rule as the only Maker of heaven and earth, and when we put aside our work on the Sabbath, including our unfinished work, and devote ourselves to worship and godly deeds, we acknowledge God as the only Creator and Redeemer and as the Lord of our lives (Exodus 31:13; Ezekiel 20:20). But this is the sign of *God's identity* and of our acknowledgment of it. Jesus taught that something else signifies our identity—that we love one another as He has loved us.

Divine love in human hearts defines who we are and whose we are. It motivates and prompts all of our deeds as workers for Christ and citizens of His kingdom. Jesus revealed the caliber of the love to which we are called by this measure: "as I have loved you." We are commanded to give to others the same love we have received from Christ. We are not to calculate whether or not our brother or sister deserves our love; none of us deserve unconditional love. In fact, the definition of grace is favor that is undeserved. This is what distinguishes the love of God from natural affection. And as we receive God's grace from the power of His love, it flows from us to others by that same power. The motivation to love doesn't lie in the person who is the object of love; it lies in the One who is the Source of love. Jesus not only loves us but desires to love others through us.

When we think of what Jesus has done for us, of all the good things we have received from His hand, we know we are under the banner of God's love. Most of all, when we think of the cross of

Christ, we know that we are loved enormously. Every one of the thousands of times Christ has forgiven us and given us a new start has come on the basis of the Cross. When we are tempted to give up and do to others what they have done to us or worse, all we have to do is remember that Jesus didn't hold our sins against us or treat us as we deserved. "As the heavens are high above the earth, so far has He removed our sins from us" (see Psalm 103:11, 12).

I remember the case of a young woman who had come back to Christ after years of living for herself. She was happy in the freedom she now had from the habits that had dominated her former life, but she was still not completely free. She was living with one remaining fear. "I know the Lord is going to make me pay for the years I was out there," she said. "I'm just waiting for it to come." It was as if she had one more hurdle to climb before she could be at peace with God and with herself. She was still holding on to guilt.

I showed her the wonderful promise God has given through His prophet Ezekiel: "When I say to the wicked, 'You will surely die,' and he turns from his sin and practices justice and righteousness, if a wicked man restores a pledge, pays back what he has taken by robbery, walks by the statutes which ensure life without committing iniquity, he shall surely live; he shall not die. *None of his sins that he has committed will be remembered against him.* He has practiced justice and righteousness; he shall surely live" (Ezekiel 33:14–16, NASB; emphasis added).

When I read to that young woman the last sentence of that passage, the promise that none of her sins would be remembered against her, a smile swept over her face, a tear rose in her eye, and she breathed a sigh of relief. In that moment she was liberated. She could stop worrying and let herself go in the Lord's love.

LOVE'S IMPLEMENTATION

"Dear children, let us not love with words or tongue but with actions and in truth" (1 John 3:18). It is through the discipline of action that God's love is exemplified in our lives; it isn't enough to be nice and talk love. Love is a principle, high and holy, and it demands our best. We must overcome our natural tendencies to self-preservation and identify ourselves with Christ's interest in other people. He was a Lover of all people, and He loved with self-sacrificing love.

Some people are hard to love, but we are not excused from the love command because of this. And in the process of sanctification, we can be sure God will bring some of these people into our lives. Some will exasperate us. They will be thoughtless, uncivilized, ignorant, obnoxious, racist, crude, hateful, and despicable, but Jesus died for all of them. Our natural reaction to such people is to look down on them, reject them, or defend ourselves against them, but—and here is the supernatural part of love—we have to deny our natural tendencies and love them better than they deserve. This is the love of Christ.

The true expression of the life of Christ in us is not that we are altruistic and perform a good deed now and then. That is human righteousness, and more often than not it is motivated by pride. The true expression of Christ in us is self-sacrificing love—the preference of others above ourselves even to our own hurt. This is how we know we have the real thing. This is how we know we are not self-deceived. "This then is how we know that we belong to the truth" (1 John 3:19). It is by laying down our lives for our brothers and sisters—not so much by dying for them, but by living sacrificially among them as Jesus lived among people when He was on the earth.

To lay down our lives means service. Every disciple of Jesus Christ has been enlisted into His service. Christian service means giving up my comfort for the sake of someone else's need. It takes the Spirit of God to live a life of service. Our nature doesn't move us to do that.

As Westerners, we have the idea that we are entitled to our comforts. We work hard, and we earn what we get, so we have the right to sit back and enjoy the fruits of our labor. We know that there are others less fortunate than we are, some who live in poverty or in deprived circumstances, but we seldom think that we might bear some responsibility for their condition. We think our being born into fortune or misfortune is fated, something that is beyond our control. And it is true that in some parts of the world there are circumstances that affect people's lives for the worst. But it hardly ever occurs to us that our good fortune makes us responsible to care for those who have been born into misfortune—that it is not an option but an obligation.

Natural resources are finite things. We share a planet on which there is only so much to go around; when people stockpile more resources than they need or can ever use, other people have to do without. In other words, in order for the privileged to live in luxury, the underprivileged must live in poverty. This perspective places the command to serve others into a new light. Service is so integral to what we are in Christ that it is not an exaggeration to say that if we have no compassion for the needs of others, we aren't living the life of the saved. The service we speak of here is not that for which we get compensation or expect to be recognized. Christian service is disinterested service, having no expectations except the glory of Christ.

COMMUNITY

God places a higher value on communal love than we generally do. At the beginning of the Christian era the believers were organized into a community so that the Son of God would have a body through which to express His life on earth. The saved community is more than just an illustration of Christ; it is, in a sense, the incarnation of Christ on the earth now, His body here in our time. To put it another way, the life of Christ in the kingdom of the world is the life of the communal body.[5]

We tend to think of Christ's promise to dwell in us by His Spirit in individual terms, each believer being possessed by the Spirit individually, and there is a sense in which this is true. But the experience of being indwelt by God's Spirit doesn't come to the disciple of Christ in isolation from the body. Paul explains it this way: that the body of Christ is "being built *together* to become a dwelling in which God lives by His Spirit" (Ephesians 2:22; emphasis added). It is the Holy Spirit living in the corporate body, not just in the individual believer.

Under the influence of individualism, the church (in the West, at least) has become more focused on personal rights and liberty than on the supremacy of the body as the expression of Christ's love in the earth. But in the community of the saved brought together by the will of God, individual identity is meant to give way to corporate reality. There is no such thing in the kingdom of Christ as a private faith or spiritual self-sufficiency. Jesus Himself, who was God in the flesh, didn't live a life of individualism, nor did He or His apostles ever teach it. When Paul described the life of the new community using the body metaphor, he emphasized not only the role of Christ as the Head of the body, but also the connection between believers as members of the body. "In Christ we who are many form one body, and each member belongs to all the others" (Romans 12:5; see also Ephesians 2:19–22; 3:17–19; 4:11–13). We would expect the apostle to say that each member belongs to Jesus, and this is true. But alongside this truth and integral to it is the truth of mutual ownership between believers. Each member belongs to all the others. We live, therefore, in a relationship of mutual responsibility for one another.

Cain had it wrong; we *are* our brother's keeper. Jesus' metaphor of the vine and the branches teaches the same life principle. As the branches must stay connected to the vine in order to have life, so the branches must also remain connected to each other in order to continue be part of the plant (John 15:1–8). The idea of mutual ownership reminds us that we are no longer to live like sheep going astray, "everyone to his own way" (Isaiah 53:6).

BROTHERHOOD

It was the fondest hope of Jesus that His disciples would learn to truly love each other. His heart's desire was for them to find in each other the same relationship that existed between the Father and Himself. This was the burden of Christ's last prayer before He went to Gethsemane (see John 17). Jesus prayed for Himself, as the time had come for the great sacrifice. He prayed for His disciples, who were about to face the most severe test of faith they would ever know. But in the last part of the prayer, Jesus prayed for us, His followers down through the ages.

The heart of that prayer on our behalf is expressed in John 17:23: "May they be brought to complete unity to let the world know that you sent me." It is interesting to notice how various translations of the Bible express this fondest hope of our Lord:

- "Be made perfect in one" (KJV).
- "Have this same kind of oneness" (*The Clear Word*).
- "Be mature in this oneness" (*The Message*).
- "Be perfected in unity" (NASB).
- "Be completely one" (NCV).
- "Be brought to complete unity" (NIV).

The imperative of brotherly love is clearly expressed not only in Jesus' prayer but throughout the whole New Testament. Paul wrote, "I pray that you, being rooted and established in love, may have power, *together with all the saints,* to grasp how wide and long and high and deep is the love of Christ, and to know this love that surpasses knowledge" (Ephesians 3:17–19; emphasis added). And Peter said, "Now that you have purified yourselves by obeying the truth so that you have sincere love for your brothers, *love one another deeply, from the heart*" (1 Peter 1:22; emphasis added). Later in his letter, he placed it in the context of earth's last days: "The end of all things is near. Therefore, be clear-minded and self-controlled so that you can pray. *Above all, love each other deeply,* because love covers a multitude of sins" (1 Peter 4:7, 8; emphasis added).

LEVELS OF RELATIONSHIP

There are at least four levels of relationship that may exist between Christian brothers and sisters, but only one of them reaches the fullness of Christ's fondest desire for His people. The first level is *rejection,* which means to discard, deny, disallow, or throw out. In truth, of course, rejection is not a relationship at all; rather it is a lack of relationship, a refusal to be in relationship. When the spirit of rejection exists between members of the body of Christ, the body is disjointed and broken. It needs attention to be made whole again.

There are times when believers reject one another based on the spirit of competition. They see each other as rivals instead of partners because of differing tastes, preferences, and even ideologies. Rejection between brothers and sisters in Christ may be rooted in rivalry and the hunger for power, in ignorance and the bigotry it fosters, or in cultural, economic, gender, or even generational differences. One of the most persistent and widespread causes of division in the church is the age-old liberal/conservative conflict. Even before we explain what we mean by these words, the labels themselves bring to mind thoughts of rivalry and competition. It almost forces one to take sides.

In this conflict, each side defends its own point of view, and neither side concerns itself with what is good for the whole. Much of the conflict between liberal and conservative Christians is over who has the right ideology and who is in the wrong. But in the light of Christ's prayer for His followers and His command that we love one another, the question becomes whether this argument should be going on in the church at all. Do the labels "liberal" and "conservative" enhance brotherhood, or are they more likely to lead to alienation and rejection? Does the church strengthen its witness or advance its mission at all by classifying itself with one or the other of these divisive terms? Even more important, when we identify ourselves by one of these labels, are we identifying with Christ? Which label fits His character? What party did He belong to when He was on the earth, or did all parties hate Him because He wouldn't identify Himself with any of them? (see Mark 3:6). Of all potential relationship between believers, the nonrelationship of rejection misrepresents Jesus more than any other.

The second level is *tolerance,* which means to forbear, to indulge, or to endure. People who are merely tolerant say in effect, "I'll put up with you, but I won't like it; my heart won't be in it. I'll grit my teeth and bear it, but I won't ever truly relax around you. And to mask my discomfort, I may even overcompensate for my lack of full acceptance of you with undue familiarity and unwarranted compliments."

Unlike rejection, tolerance is a form of relationship, but not a positive one. The most we can say in favor of this kind of relationship is that it is better than rejection, though not much better. When we tolerate others we won't do anything to harm them, but we won't do anything to help them either. Some people adopt this posture because someone from another culture or gender or generation has offended them in the past and they haven't gotten over it. The offense may even go back generations, but they hold on to it and vent their rage upon an entire group rather than treating each person on his or her own merits and showing them the dignity and respect they deserve.

When we tolerate others, we never really open our hearts to them. The people we tolerate can tell that we don't really like them. They can tell when our friendship is only superficial. Our discomfort comes through no matter how we try to mask it. We can't fake our way into genuine relationship; we must pray past our pains and ask God for a changed heart.

The third level is *acceptance,* acknowledging, recognizing, or approving someone. People who accept others in effect say, "I realize

I've been wrong in keeping you at a distance, in not attempting to get to know you, in treating you as a category instead of a unique person. I acknowledge you as a son [or a daughter] of God. I accept you as you are at all times, not just when you comply with my expectations. I accept your differences, and I'll sit beside you, share a meal with you, listen to your music, and let you speak in your own language. I'll relax and stop trying to impress you with my open-mindedness and instead truly open my mind to you and to what I can learn from you," and just like that, genuine relationship appears.

Acceptance is a big step toward Christian relationship. It means that I have given up trying to prove the superiority of my group and have decided to make myself vulnerable to you. I know that this vulnerability may be used against me, but I have determined by the grace of God to risk it for Jesus' sake. No longer are the differences between us a barrier; rather, they become the means of a greater appreciation for the diversity of the body and a better understanding of its unity (1 Corinthians 12:12). Accepting one another doesn't mean that we overlook our differences; it means that we love each other as we are, with all of our differences. We don't pressure the other person to be like us when we're together, and that means we don't feel we must hide our preferences while in each other's company. When we accept one another, we are comfortable being our true selves when we are together because we see each other through the eyes of the love of Christ.

As important a step as this is in the realizing of true brotherhood, however, it still doesn't answer Jesus' prayer of John 17. Even acceptance of each other doesn't reach the zenith of the love for one another our Lord had in mind for us. It is a start, but it isn't the finish. There is a category of relationship that is better still.

The fourth level is *nurture*—to care for, look after, encourage, and support someone else. Nurture is an expression of love that doesn't merely receive the other; it pours itself out for the other. It doesn't simply accept; it seeks. Nurturing love not only acknowledges the other, it sacrifices itself for the other. We seldom reach this depth in our relationships, especially when those relationships cross cultural lines or differences in position, power, or education. We may tolerate, we may even grow to accept each other without discrimination, but very rarely do we nurture another the way we nurture our own, or elevate another to a station above ourselves (Romans 12:10).

When I love you with a nurturing love, I don't just sit beside you, I sit *with* you. I don't just share in a meal, I learn about your food. I don't just open my mind to you, I open my heart. Consequently, when you suffer, I suffer, and when you rejoice, I rejoice, as though we were two parts of the same body (1 Corinthians 12:26, 27). And when I love you with a nurturing love—and this is important—I don't keep silent when someone from my group maligns you because you belong to another group. You and I belong to the same group now, and any offense against you is an offense against me (1 Corinthians 12:22, 23). So I stand up for you as my brother or sister in Christ even when you aren't present to hear it. I even confront my own family members when they are in the wrong. I never leave you to fend for yourself; I take your part against those who are threatening the body of Christ by attacking you with hurtful words or attitudes.

THE MOST IMPORTANT COMMANDMENTS

On one of the few occasions—if not the only one—when the scribes agreed with Jesus, it was regarding the commandments of God, and specifically, which was the most important commandment. Perhaps the consensus between them was not so remarkable; the great commandment was one of the most time-honored oracles of Hebrew tradition going back to Moses. Jesus was quoting from the books of Moses when He identified the two most important commandments— "Love the Lord your God with all your heart and with all your soul," and "Love your neighbor as yourself" (Mark 12:30, 31; compare Deuteronomy 6:4, 5; Leviticus 19:18).

It is worth noting that in Christ's response to the question regarding the great commandment, though He combined the two texts as one, He labeled the commandment regarding the neighbor as "the second," suggesting that it was not as important as the first, which was love to God. This is no surprise. God always belongs in first place.

We *are* surprised, then, at the realization that when, years later, the apostle Paul condensed the Ten Commandments into one command, the one he omitted was the first, the one regarding love to God, not the second, the one calling us to love our neighbors. He said, "The commandments, 'Do not commit adultery,' 'Do not murder,' 'Do not steal,' 'Do not covet,' and whatever other commandment there may be, are summed up in *this one rule*: 'Love your neighbor as yourself' " (Romans 13:9; emphasis added). "The entire law is summed up in *a single command:* 'Love your neighbor as yourself' " (Galatians 5:14; emphasis added).

What's going on?

Was Paul taking liberties with Christ's teachings? Christ had plainly said that the commandments of God are summed up in two loves—we're to love God and to love our neighbor, and in that order. Clearly, He was referencing the Old Testament, which had stood for thousands of years. But Paul reduced God's imperative from two commandments to one.

Right away, then, we know that we must look for a deeper meaning, since the Word of God doesn't contradict itself. And when we look into it further, what appears to be a contradiction turns out to be a progression, an advancement of truth that is consistent throughout. Paul's theology of love is nothing more than a restatement of the teaching of Jesus as it developed after the Cross. The two loves of the great commandment are expressed as one in the context of the new community in Christ. Here is the final, emphatic endorsement of the brotherhood mandate of John's first letter: "If anyone says, 'I love God,' yet hates his brother, he is a liar. For anyone who does not love his brother, whom he has seen, cannot love God, whom he has not seen. And he has given us this command: Whoever loves God must also love his brother" (1 John 4:20, 21).

Now we can piece the puzzle together and see the harmony between the declarations made by Jesus and Paul. In the New Testament pattern, the apostles in their letters explain the teachings of Jesus, which are recorded in the Gospels. In this case, Jesus states the two commandments, and Paul explains that the two are actually one.

Paul's reduction of the two great commandments down to one is a lesson on how Christ's love functions. The two commandments are intimately related: love to God and love to neighbor cannot, in fact, be separated; the one has everything to do with the other—so much so that neither can exist without the other. To truly love God is to love your brother and your sister. "The spirit we manifest toward our brethren declares what is our spirit toward God. The love of God in the heart is the only spring of love toward our neighbor."[6]

Robert Mulholland translates the Mark 12 pronouncement of Jesus in a way that shows this connection: "You shall love the Lord your God with all your heart, and with all your soul, and with all your mind, and with all your strength. *Another way to say the same thing is,* 'you shall love your neighbor as yourself.' "[7]

We reveal whether or not we love God by whether or not we love our neighbors. Love cannot help but express itself in acts of compassion and self-sacrifice, which is exactly what is needed in a sinful world where suffering abounds. Professing to love God while not showing love toward one's neighbors is a waste of breath. Anyone can claim to love an invisible God, but when we "lay down our lives for our brothers . . . this then is how we know that we belong to the truth" (1 John 3:16, 19).

In his book on the gospel of Jesus, Henri Nouwen raises the issue of what he calls "a forgotten question"[8]—an interesting concept that he directs at believers. He points out that many Christians live as though the question they expect to hear in the judgment is "How much money did you make?" or "How far did you go in school?" or "How famous did you become?" According to Jesus, though, we will face only one question in the judgment: "What have you done for the least of these?"

Some believe that God is going to judge them by how well they kept the religious regulations, but that isn't what Jesus meant by commandment keeping. That isn't what obedience to Christ signifies. We picture the law of God as written on two tables of stone, but the nature of the law is not stone but spirit. The law is spiritual. We can never satisfy its claims if we're trying to do so outwardly, with no inner change. *Love* is the only fulfillment of the law.

BACK TO CAIN AND ABEL

Cain and Abel had both been taught the meaning of the sacrificial system. Adam taught his sons the significance of the lamb on the altar, which symbolized innocence, obedience, total dependence on God, and most importantly, the Redeemer to come. But Cain rebelled against God, blaming Him for the curse of sin. His decision to put produce on the altar was a sign of rebellion—his refusal to submit to anyone, including God. The motives that led him to murder his brother were the same as those that prompted his kind of worship: rebellion, pride, and self-exaltation. These are the things that made Cain's worship unacceptable to God.[9] It is of critical importance that we understand this.

We live in the time of the outpouring of God's Spirit in latter-rain power, and as a church, we realize how desperately we need it. But we can't receive the latter rain if we haven't fulfilled the conditions of the early rain. Of that outpouring of the Spirit, Scripture says, "When the day of Pentecost had fully come, they were all with one accord in one place" (Acts 2:1, NKJV).

The accord that the disciples experienced just before the outpouring of the Holy Spirit in the first century was not just a coming together in one location; it was a coming together into one heart and mind through surrender to Jesus and His love. The togetherness of the upper room was both geographical and interpersonal. The original language of Acts 2:1 may be translated this way: "When the Day of Pentecost was completed they were all together, together"—two comings together, not just one. As the disciples drew closer to Jesus, they drew closer to each other. And this accord, this oneness of Christ's followers in which all rivalry and desire for power was suspended, opened the way for God's Spirit to be poured out, which resulted in the gospel of Jesus going forward with spectacular results.

"The disciples prayed with intense earnestness for a fitness to meet men and in their daily intercourse to speak words that would lead sinners to Christ. Putting away all differences, all desire for the supremacy, they came close together in Christian fellowship."[10] Since that hallowed beginning, the Christian church hasn't maintained the community that marked its debut on the Day of Pentecost. Now is the time for us to seek that brotherhood again with our whole hearts. "Again and again the angel has said to me, 'Press together, press together, be of one mind, of one judgment,' Christ is the leader, and you are brethren; follow Him."[11]

South African bishop Desmond Tutu's Truth and Reconciliation Commission has unearthed some shocking stories of depraved deeds done when apartheid was the official policy of the government. One black South African woman sat in a courtroom and listened as a white police officer acknowledged his part in the murder of her son. In open court, he said that he had shot the eighteen-year-old at point-blank range and then partied with other officers as they burned his body, turning it over and over in the flames until nothing was left but ashes. Eight years later, the policeman said, he returned with other officers and seized the woman's husband. This time she was forced to watch as they bound him on a woodpile, poured gasoline over his body, and burned him alive. The last words she heard her husband say were, "Forgive them!"

After relating his horrendous story, Officer Van de Broek awaited judgment. The judge turned to the widowed woman and asked her what sentence she thought should be handed down. "I want three things," she said. "First, I want Officer Van de Broek to take me to the place where they burned my husband's body so I may gather his ashes and give him a decent burial. Second, since my family is gone and I have so much love to give, I want Mr. Van de Broek to come to the ghetto twice a month and spend the day with me so that I can be a mother to him. Third, I would like Mr. Van de Broek to know that God forgives him and that I forgive him too. And so that he can know my forgiveness is real, I would like to embrace him right now."

With that, the old woman started across the courtroom, and Van de Broek began to tremble. Someone began singing "Amazing Grace," the entire courtroom joined in, and the officer, overwhelmed by the power of forgiving love that permeated that courtroom, fainted on the witness stand.[12] This is the power that belongs to the church based on Christ's redeeming love. The Spirit of God longs for us to claim this power as our own.

"When men are bound together, not by force or self-interest, but by love, they show the working of an influence that is above every human influence. Where this oneness exists, it is evidence that the image of God is being restored in humanity, that a new principle of life has been implanted."[13]

HOLINESS: ENOCH
CHAPTER 4

Just as he who called you is holy, so be holy in all you do.
—1 Peter 1:15

As Adam and Eve mournfully began the life of the fallen, they experienced things God never intended humans to know. They witnessed the degeneration of the created order under the curse of sin. Weather patterns changed, adding extremes of hot and cold. Plants wilted, faded, and died. Animals became more competitive and ferocious, some of them becoming predatory, threatening human beings and feeding on the other animals instead of eating the vegetation provided by the Creator. And worst of all, every living thing became subject to death. As we noted regarding moral depravity in chapter 2, it could be said of Adam and Eve that they became "not able not to sin." It is also true that in the physical sense they became "not able not to die." They had been created with conditional immortality, which was dependent on access to the tree of life. When they lost that access, they became mortal—subject to injury, aging, disease, and death.

Being rebels against God was a new experience, and Adam and Eve didn't fully understand all of the implications. What happened to the world after they had taken the forbidden fruit must have been a shameful surprise. But our first parents' fall into sin had enormous consequences for them too. The instant they became sinners they experienced an internal degradation at the most basic level. They were fundamentally changed in a way they couldn't reverse or repair or even fully comprehend. They still looked like themselves—beings made in the image of God, but now the image was marred and their spirits were damaged. They began to act on the basis of the new reality, the reality of sin, and in their actions we perceive the attributes that we inherited as their sons and daughters.

Human nature is multifaceted, a holistic composition of three integrated parts: spirit, soul, and body (see Genesis 2:7; 1 Thessalonians 5:23). The dichotomous philosophy of the Greeks—the idea that human nature is composed of a soul trapped in a body and waiting to escape through mysticism or death—is not taught in Scripture. The Bible gives no indication that any aspect of our being is independently conscious. Human nature is built on the model of the Triune God, the One in whose image we were created, and the three aspects of our nature are integrated just as Father, Son, and Holy Ghost are One. However, just as the Members of the Godhead can be distinguished from One Another even though God is One, so also the three aspects of human nature can be distinguished even though they are holistically interrelated and interdependent.

Some of what we are about to consider will be difficult to conceptualize —that is, to form into something concrete that we can picture. We must be ready to think abstractly, and we must be willing to take the time to digest these thoughts fully. And when a physical object is used as an analogy, we will have to keep in mind that analogies are tools of comparison that, when pushed too far, end up distorting the very thing they were meant to clarify.

In what follows, I want to explore the theology of Watchman Nee, explaining the scriptural view of the human makeup as groundwork for understanding the divine holiness.[1]

THE NATURE OF OUR BEING

Human nature is described in Scripture as tripartite, an integrated unity of three components: spirit, soul, and body. The body is our outer shell, the material part of our being made from the "dust of the ground." As bodily creatures, we have a physical aspect—we're made of physical matter; we have flesh and blood. This is the obvious part of our nature, the part that enables us to live in the physical world. We interact with the world through our bodily senses: hearing, sight, smell, taste, and touch. But in our fallen condition, with the spirit—

our "higher" nature—dead through sin (Ephesians 2:1, 2), the body rules when it was meant to be subservient. The desires and cravings of the body take control of our lives. We have fallen below our original standing as beings made in the divine image and have instead become like the animals—"brute beasts, creatures of instinct, born only to be caught and destroyed" (2 Peter 2:12).

This is the tyranny of the body in sin. Its drives and cravings assert themselves against our will and make us captive to whatever behavior brings bodily satisfaction, brief and transitory though it be. Who of us has not known this tyranny of the flesh in the habits of life we have struggled against, in some cases for our whole lives? Paul named them:

> Now the works of the flesh are evident, which are: adultery, fornication, uncleanness, lewdness, idolatry, sorcery, hatred, contentions, jealousies, outbursts of wrath, selfish ambitions, dissensions, heresies, envy, murders, drunkenness, revelries, and the like; of which I tell you beforehand, just as I also told you in time past, that those who practice such things will not inherit the kingdom of God (Galatians 5:19–21, NKJV).

The only way to escape this tyranny is to put the body to death by identifying with Christ in His death. "Our old man was crucified with Him, that the body of sin might be done away with, that we should no longer be slaves of sin. For he who has died has been freed from sin" (Romans 6:6, 7, NKJV). So the Lord says that we must present our bodies to Him as living sacrifices and that even in our brokenness, the gift of ourselves will please Him (Romans 12:1).

The soul—brought into being when the breath of God reacted with the dust of the ground out of which the body was formed—is the inward part of our nature by which we express individuality through our intellect, emotions, and will. The soul is the seat of personality. It is the source of rationality—of our ability to think, reason, reflect, and comprehend. It is also the place of emotion, the part of our nature through which we express our likes and dislikes as joy or sorrow, laughter or tears. It was in His soul that Jesus felt the profound melancholy produced by the weight of the world's sin—an emotion so deep that it caused Him to exclaim, "My soul is overwhelmed with sorrow *to the point of death*" (Matthew 26:38; emphasis added). In order for Christ to reign in us, we must submit our souls to God's rule of the spirit.

THE SPIRIT IN CONTROL

When we are made whole again through reconciliation with Jesus Christ, our emotions, our thought processes, and even our sense of individuality all come under the control of our spirit. This submission of the soul to the spirit in us is especially important as we seek to offer true worship to God, the One who is Spirit (John 4:24). When the soul is the ruling force in worship, its attributes shape our worship. Instead of worshiping God "in Spirit and in truth," our worship is guided principally either by our rational powers—which results in cerebral, intellectual worship—or by our feeling powers—which results in emotional, charismatic worship.

In the first instance, the worshipers feel blessed when their intellect is stimulated. Their response to worship is contemplative and stoical, involving little or no emotion. They may even suppress emotion in an effort to find what for them is "true worship." They value refined music and mildly academic sermons compatible with an "enlightened" and rationalistic culture—a "high church" form of worship that they consider to be superior.

In the second instance, the worshipers feel blessed when their emotions run high during the worship service—when the ecstatic and rapturous elements are prominent. They tend to interpret high emotion as spiritual power, just as the rational worshipers interpret intellectualism as spiritual perception. The emotional worshipers may even seek to stir up vocal and demonstrative responses in themselves or in others, considering those responses to be the sign of genuine worship. They consider their worship practice to be superior because it is "spiritual church."

Jesus' statement to the Samaritan woman that "true worshipers will worship the Father in spirit and in truth" (John 4:23) suggests that neither of these approaches is in complete harmony with God's will for His people. Because by nature we are holistic beings, all of our powers participate together in the worship experience. We are rational and emotional beings, and we don't need to abandon either of these attributes in our worship of God. But in order to offer to God the worship He requires, our praise and thanksgiving must emanate from our spirits, not from our souls. We must study what it means to worship God with our whole being, not in intellectualism or emotionalism but "in spirit and in truth."

Spirit is the innermost aspect of human nature, beyond self-consciousness. We comprehend Christ's teachings through our soul powers; we obey Christ and take part in His mission on the earth with our bodies; but we know Jesus Christ, we know that He is real even though we have never seen Him, through the attributes of our spirits— His Spirit testifying with our spirit that we are the children of God (Romans 8:16). "His Spirit searches out everything and shows us God's deep secrets. No one can know a person's thoughts except that person's own spirit, and no one can know God's thoughts except God's own Spirit" (1 Corinthians 2:10, 11, NLT).

We are capable of knowing God. We *can* know Him, which is why atheism must be expressed as a negation. (The Greek root of the word literally means "no God.") Yet in order to escape our fears that one day we will have to answer to God, we try to erase the reality that can never be erased—the reality of God.

The human spirit is the primary battlefield of the great controversy between Christ and Satan. It is here that the enemy desires to plant his flag of control over us, and it is here that the Spirit of God makes His appeal for us to surrender willingly to Christ in love. Christ wants us to give ourselves freely to Him in the same way as He gave Himself freely for us. Nothing in the universe is more important to Jesus than that we freely choose to live in intimate relationship with Him because we love Him and that we live out that relationship through the obedience of faith.

Paul was speaking of the battle between Christ and Satan that takes place in the human spirit when he wrote, "We wrestle not against flesh and blood" (Ephesians 6:12, KJV). It is there that our salvation or condemnation is determined. There is no teacher in the world, however skilled and distinguished, who can change a person's spirit. Books and learning cannot change the inward desires and hidden motives. Education cannot cure the plague of a self-centered, self-directed human heart or the guilt it carries under the load of unresolved sin. It is only when people are born from above, with the resultant change of desires, that their spirits no longer hanker for sin but pant after God instead (John 3:3). Only the Spirit of the Lord can transform us from sinners into saints; only the still, small Voice draws us back to God so our original relationship with Him can be restored.

ENOCH

When we think of the development of the spiritual life to its full potential, our thoughts turn to an Old Testament character: Enoch, the seventh from Adam. Four thousand years before the manger of Bethlehem, Jesus of Nazareth was foreshadowed in the life of this man who walked with God, who did nothing of his own self, who sought not to please himself but to please God only. Before Balaam's oracle about the star out of Jacob and the scepter from Israel, Jesus' rule over the kingdom of hell could already be seen in the life of Enoch. This son of Adam was the first whose life showed that the enmity between the snake and the woman was firmly established, thus giving the assurance that one day the serpent's head would surely be crushed.

This child who would become unique among the patriarchs for the depth of his relationship with God was born in Adam's 622nd year. At the time of his birth, there was no sign of what he would become. He was born in sin just as were all those before him and after him. He grew into manhood, married a woman, and established a home of his own as most every man who comes of age desires to do. But when he had a son, Methuselah, and began to experience fatherhood for the first time, he understood better the fatherhood of God and entered into a new level of relationship with his heavenly Father.

Enoch kept God in the forefront of his mind at all times, relating everything in his life, even the mundane things, to Him, discarding everything that would distract him from God. Thus he dwelt in heavenly places even while he lived in human society. After he became the father of Methuselah, he walked even more closely with God and became complete in holiness—so much so that God brought him home ahead of schedule, and "Enoch walked with God; then he was no more, because God took him away" (Genesis 5:24).

How does a person walk with God?

Rarely do we as adults give any consideration to ordinary walking.

After a while, it comes so easily as to be almost involuntary, so we tend to take it for granted. But for infants and the disabled, walking is a challenging and highly prized ability.

Walking with God doesn't come naturally either—every believer must learn how to do it, and the learning process can be difficult. Like a little child just beginning to learn the physical skill, we often fall spiritually and get bumps and bruises as a result, so it can be discouraging at times. But if we never exercise our spiritual muscles, if we just give up and never learn to live our faith consistently, we eventually become stagnant, inoperative, "couch potato" Christians, and we lose our place with God.

To learn to walk means to move along on foot, to make headway, to advance by steps. It is growth as opposed to stagnation; action as opposed to mere theorizing. To walk with someone may also mean to continue in union with that person. In that sense, it means fellowship as opposed to individualism; agreement rather than opposition. So we see that the metaphor of walking has deep implications for the spiritual life.

NOT BY OUR OWN POWER

Jesus made it clear that apart from Him, we have no spiritual life. He said, "I am the way and the truth and the life. No one comes to the Father except through me" (John 14:6), and "I am the vine; you are the branches. He who abides in Me, and I in him, will bear much fruit; for without Me you can do nothing" (John 15:5, NKJV).

The second text draws an example from nature. In the natural order, plants don't grow by their own care or anxiety but by receiving what God has furnished. It is the air, the sunshine, and the nutrients in the soil that support growth. Plants must depend upon God to supply what they need but cannot produce. They are completely dependent upon the Creator.

Similarly, we can't grow in grace through our own willpower or works—even righteous works. Many have the idea that there is some part of the work of salvation they must do on their own, that after they come to Christ, they must learn to stand on their own two feet. But we can't supply what we must have to grow in grace. We can't produce those necessities, we can only receive them.

Jesus said, "No one comes to the Father except through Me," and

He said, "He who abides in Me bears much fruit." The prepositions He used in these two sentences are important. In the first, Jesus says *"through* Me," and in the second, He says *"in* Me." These words reflect both submission and intimacy. You don't just walk *with* Me, says Jesus, but *in* Me and *through* Me. He is talking about a greater closeness than merely walking side by side. People who walk beside each other maintain some degree of independence. But in order to walk *through* another person or *in* that person, we must give up our independence altogether and become completely dependent on the other. Here we see the new life that we must learn to live—the life of a self that is lost in Christ.

"As you have received Christ Jesus the Lord, so walk in Him, having been firmly rooted and now being built up in Him and established in your faith, just as you were instructed, and overflowing with gratitude" (Colossians 2:6, 7, NASB). We must give up the idea that we can walk with God while clinging to our individual rights and freedoms. Everything associated with our nature has been corrupted by sin; there is no good side in us that we can keep. The walk with God in Jesus Christ calls for a complete denial of one's self and a conscious building inside us of the life Christ gives. Paul told the Colossians, "You died, and your life is hidden with Christ in God" (Colossians 3:3, NKJV). Then he added, "When Christ who is our life, appears, then you also will appear with Him in glory. Therefore put to death your members which are on the earth" (verses 4, 5, NKJV). We cannot walk with God in our own power.

NOT WHILE ENGAGING IN KNOWN SIN

The deliberate practice of known sin is the biggest threat to our spiritual lives. Paul enumerated some of the practices that those who walk with God must leave behind as we take God's hand to walk with Him. We are to have nothing to do with immorality, impurity, greed, anger, slander, filthy language, and lying. These things belong to our fallen nature, and God will surely reject them. To deliberately continue in known sin with no intention of stopping puts us on the path to eternal separation from God—the path to eternal death. Both the Old and the New Testaments warn us against taking that course, using the experience of Israel in the wilderness as an example.

Recording the Lord's words, one of the psalmists wrote,

Today, if you hear his voice,
    do not harden your hearts as you did at Meribah. . . .
For forty years I was angry with that generation;
I said, "They are a people whose hearts go astray,
    and they have not known my ways."
So I declared on oath in my anger,
    "They shall never enter my rest" (Psalm 95:7, 8, 10, 11).

And they never did. That rebellious generation died in the wilderness, and their children got the reward that God intended the older generation to have. They epitomized people who remain stiff-necked after many rebukes. The Bible says that such people will be destroyed suddenly without remedy (Proverbs 29:1). In the story of Israel, we hear the first sounding of an ominous note that reverberates through the rest of the Bible, all the way to the end of the New Testament. We can so resist the Spirit of God that we damage our spirit in a way that eliminates the possibility of repair; then we are "without remedy." The Bible clearly teaches that no power on earth or in hell can pluck us out of Christ's hand once we have come to Him. But we always have the power to take ourselves out of His hand by the choices we make, especially those we repeat continuously. Note the following warnings:

- "Because of your stubbornness and your unrepentant heart, you are storing up wrath against yourself for the day of God's wrath, when His righteous judgment will be revealed" (Romans 2:5).
- "Encourage one another daily, as long as it is called Today, so that none of you may be hardened by sin's deceitfulness" (Hebrews 3:13).
- "If we deliberately keep on sinning after we have received the knowledge of the truth, no sacrifice for sins is left, but only a fearful expectation of judgment and of raging fire that will consume the enemies of God" (Hebrews 10:26, 27).

It is no longer fashionable and may even be viewed as archaic and ignorant to talk about hellfire. Some of the pioneers of Christian preaching harped on the subject so frequently that people turned away from it. And it's true that people cannot be converted to Christ by the fear of damnation. Fear may cause people to change their behavior, but only love can change the heart. However, it is also true that the Bible contains many warnings that the wrath of God will certainly come to those who finally reject His Son, so we must not make the fatal mistake of thinking that because God's judgments do not appear here and now, they will never come. God will judge the world in righteousness and destroy all sin. We must, by the grace of God, rid our lives of all known and deliberate sin now, before our hearts become so hardened that grace can no longer work effectively in our lives.

I read an unusual story about a woman named Mary Strey who called 911 to report a drunk driver. When the dispatcher asked her if she was following the driver, she said, her speech slurred, "The driver is me."

The dispatcher instructed Mary to pull over, turn off the engine, turn on the car's flashers, and wait for the police to come. When they arrived, they arrested her and charged her with drunk driving. In essence, then, Mary had herself arrested! An online respondent who, in trying to understand put herself in Mary's place, commented, "It sounds like she didn't realize how drunk she was until she started driving, and [she] didn't want to continue."

We can learn something about the spiritual walk from this story. Our spiritual walk depends on the deliberate act of turning ourselves in. We call that act *repentance*—our confession of sin and turning away from it. In the life of believers who are walking with God, repentance is not just an occasional act; it is a basic constituent of the life.

ENOCH'S SECRET

The connection between Enoch's fatherhood and his walk with God was not a coincidence. Becoming a father had a profound effect on Enoch. Through experiencing the father-son relationship, he learned the meaning of divine love for lost humanity. He realized in a new way how much God loved him and what it meant to love God in return. And by extension, we see in Enoch's experience the important role the home plays in redemption, and the reason that Satan is so intent on breaking up our marriages and alienating parents from their children and children from their parents. If it is true that the experience of parenthood has the potential of opening our eyes to God's holiness, it follows that the tragedy of the broken home can cause us to forget God and lose our connection to Him.

So what was Enoch's secret? How did he become so close to God as to live a holy life, walking with God continually without losing step and without becoming separated? Jesus employed the metaphor of the vine and the branches to explain the only way in which this happens for any believer: "No branch can bear fruit by itself; it must remain in the vine" (John 15:4). "I am the vine, you are the branches. He who abides in Me, and I in him, bears much fruit; for without Me you can do nothing" (verse 5, NKJV).

Someone may ask, "What does it mean to abide in Christ and to live the life of the spirit?" Enoch exemplifies the answer. A spiritual person is one who is always conscious of the presence of God and who lives in response to God's presence. We don't obtain holiness through rationality or emotionalism. Spiritual growth isn't something we reason or calculate into being. In fact, it isn't something we do but something that God's Spirit does in us. The claim of God upon our lives is not merely that we should be moral and ethical persons, but that we should be holy as God is holy. We will reach this goal only when we have the relationship to which we are called. Both the calling and the accomplishment have the same Source. "Just as he who called you is holy, so be holy in all you do; for it is written: 'Be holy, because I am holy' " (1 Peter 1:15, 16). "And we, who with unveiled faces all reflect the Lord's glory, are being transformed into his likeness with ever-increasing glory, which comes from the Lord, who is the Spirit" (2 Corinthians 3:18).

Paul is not saying that we transform ourselves. Rather, as we look to Jesus and abide in Him, we are being transformed by the Holy Spirit. Holiness is God's work within us by His Spirit. The Holy Spirit performs the transformation, which we have no idea how to do nor what the final product looks like. But as we confess the Lord Jesus Christ and keep our lives centered in Him, we are changed into exactly what God wants us to be. This transformation progresses for the rest of our lives—that is what it means to "walk with God."

What God would have us do is plainly set before us, but we must remember that it happens in the context of the great controversy. We will meet resistance as we attempt to live for Jesus and abide in Him. The resistance will come both from the world outside of us, which is full of sin, and from inside of us, from our fallen natures. We have something to do—we have a role in overcoming as we pursue holiness in Christ. But there's an assurance for us: if Enoch walked with God in an exceedingly wicked generation, so can we. Jesus said that if we'll abide in Him, He'll abide in us. He won't fail us if we trust Him and let Him take charge of our life.

ENOCH AND THE LAST DAYS

Ellen White's comments regarding the characteristics and habits of Enoch's life as he progressed toward holiness are instructive: "His conversation was on heavenly things. He educated his mind to run in this channel"; "he did not make his abode with the wicked"; "Enoch was a man of strong and highly cultivated mind"; "he instructed [people] and prayed for them"; "He chose certain periods for retirement . . . from all society"; "he was one of the humblest of men"; "He was a representative of the saints who live amid the perils and corruptions of the last days."[2]

Notice especially the final observation: Enoch was a prototype of God's people of the last days—the people who expect to receive the seal of God in the time of the mark of the beast. God's people of the end time will fulfill their mission and triumph over the enemy only as they learn to do what Enoch did—to walk continually with God.

We are now in that time, and we won't be able to withstand the test of the last days if our faith is superficial, halfhearted, or focused only on outward behavior. We must appropriate the law of God into our hearts and lives. Paul wrote of this in the book of Hebrews, quoting Jeremiah's prophecy: "This is the covenant I will make with the house of Israel after that time, declares the Lord. I will put my laws in their minds and write them on their hearts. I will be their God, and they will be my people" (Hebrews 8:10).

All Christians must choose individually into whose hands they will place their minds and hearts. This much is certain; no one who ends up in hell will be able to say, "God put me here," and no one who ends up in heaven will be able to say, "I put myself here."

For years the United Negro College Fund has used a slogan to promote education, one that is both profound and true: "A mind is a terrible thing to waste." However, it is also true that people can waste an educated mind, even a highly educated mind. Education can be used for good or for evil. It can be used to bless the world or to use the world selfishly. In some ways, the latter is a worse waste than it is to be ignorant all of one's life.

The secret of walking with God isn't found in the feet, but in the mind. Jesus has a claim upon our minds that no one else can match or even approach. He has redeemed us by His own life, and our response to Him must be total—spirit, soul, and body.

Lon Perry was an unusual thief whom the police called "the Gentleman Bandit."[3] Over a period of two years, he committed more than one hundred robberies in Texas and Louisiana, mainly in hotel rooms.

Perry got his nickname because of the unusual way he operated: He always treated his victims with impeccable manners. He said "please" and "thank you" while he held people at gunpoint, and "excuse me" as he rifled through their purses and wallets. He was known to return by mail his victims' photos of their grandchildren and to phone them later to ask how they were recovering from their ordeal. On one occasion, concerned about the condition of a victim he had tied up, he called the front desk of the hotel and reported, "The person in room 319 could use some help." He also wrote down his victims' names and addresses with the promise that he would pay them back some day.

When Perry finally was arrested, the authorities discovered he was a churchgoing family man with two children who had lost his job as a computer programmer for an oil company and consequently had fallen on hard times. He was discovered only because he turned himself in to prevent another man from going to prison—a man who was being charged with committing Perry's crimes. Surprisingly, many of Perry's victims were genuinely sorry that he had been caught. One man said, "He was so kind I just gave him my money," and a woman he had robbed said, "If I ever get robbed again, I would want it to be by him."

Kindness and consideration touch us deeply, even when their source is a thief who's robbing us. How much more powerful is the perfect grace that comes from the heart of God! We underestimate what this power can do in our lives. It is the source of the victory over sin that holiness represents, the victory that is our destiny as we abide in Christ and walk with God just as Enoch did.

SALVATION: NOAH'S ARK
CHAPTER 5

Noah found grace in the eyes of the LORD.
—Genesis 6:8, KJV

Because of the limits of human perception, railroad crossings are more dangerous than we generally realize. We can't accurately judge how fast a train is moving—a real-world instance of "seeing is not believing." The problem is that trains seem to be going half as fast as they actually are, and they're half the distance from us that they appear to be. In other words, a train that's going sixty miles per hour and is half a mile away looks as though it's going thirty miles an hour and is a mile away. And trains are enormous: a freight train of one hundred loaded cars may weigh twelve million pounds and take a full mile to come to a complete stop.[1] The point is, don't mess with a moving train!

The same principle applies to life on a dangerous planet, and in fact, the peril we face here is even greater than that posed by trains because not only are our bodies at stake, but our souls are too. Jesus Christ is our only hope of avoiding the eternal destruction that otherwise would be the inevitable result of our colliding with sin. Noah, who lived through the world's first universal crisis, shows us how God saves people from the danger sin poses.

A WICKED WORLD

God warned Noah that something much more dangerous than a freight train was coming down the track. He said, "I am going to put an end to all people, for the earth is filled with violence because of them. I am surely going to destroy both them and the earth. So make yourself an ark of cypress wood" (Genesis 6:13, 14). Scripture speaks of three arks—no, make that four arks—that God used either as symbols of or as the literal means of salvation. Noah's ark was the first. This is the story of that ark, and of its builder.

In Noah's day, the world had become full of wickedness and violence. Genesis 4 concludes with a view of the contrast between two divergent lines within the human family, one known as "the sons of God," the other "the sons of men." It is not without significance that the seventh generation of each line reached the highest expression of its tendencies, seven being the biblical number of completion.[2] The seventh from Adam in the line of Cain, the world's first murderer, was the godless Lamech, son of Methushael. He was the veritable incarnation of self-sufficient pride, the man who invented bigamy. In the one utterance of his that Scripture records, his character leaps to view in bold relief. With remorseless rebellion he proclaimed, "I have killed a man for wounding me, a young man for injuring me."[3] A true descendant of Cain, Lamech was proud to be a murderer, and he feared neither God nor God's judgment.

The seventh from Adam in the line of Seth was the godly Enoch, son of Jared. Enoch was so in step with God that the divine nature was reproduced in him. He was the first "son of God" whose relationship with the Creator became so perfected that even in the midst of a wicked generation, his natural tendencies harmonized completely with the Divine. The image of God was so totally restored in Enoch that the metaphor "Enoch walked with God" became literally true. He was the first human to enter heaven.

As the generations passed, the two genealogical lines intermingled through marriage, and consequently, the wickedness of humankind became more pronounced. By the tenth generation, things had gotten so bad that only the most severe language could describe the depraved condition of human beings and the awesome grief of God. One translation put it this way: "Every idea of the plans of his mind was nothing but evil all the time."[4]

The Hebrew verb for "evil" connotes molding something like a potter molds clay, and the word translated "mind" is literally "heart," which in biblical symbolism represents the soul, the center of human thought, emotion, and will. The point is that from its very source, every human impulse is innately and thoroughly evil, with not the slightest good.[5] This represents what happens to all of us without the intervention of God. This is what we all would be were it not for God's restraining Spirit and His gracious work of redemption in the life of believers. Human nature is overpowered by sin until we can do nothing but sin. This is what became of the world in Noah's time.

So the Lord God resolved to blot out the work of His own hands, His sons and daughters whom He loved, and the thought broke His heart. But there was one bright spot. He wouldn't doom everyone to destruction. "Noah found grace in the eyes of the LORD" (Genesis 6:8, NKJV).

THE DOOR

Noah and his family were charter members of the remnant church, the last people on earth who were still serving God at that time. They lived through the world's first "time of trouble" and made it safely to the Promised Land. And it was the ark that carried them through troubled waters.

God's grace to Noah and his family required a vehicle, a means of transport by which salvation could be conveyed. That vehicle was the ark, which has been a symbol of salvation ever since. By studying it, we learn more about how salvation comes through Jesus Christ.

God told Noah to "put a door in the side of the ark and make lower, middle and upper decks" (Genesis 6:16). Notice that not only was there just one ark, but that one ark had just one door, one way in—*and Noah didn't have the key.* One door only, to be opened and shut by God alone. That single door, the one way into the ark, represents Jesus Christ Himself, who said, "I am the door; by me if any man enter in, he shall be saved" (John 10:9, KJV). The fact that God's plan for the ark called for only one door, only one way to safety, symbolized that there is only one way of salvation.

Though Genesis records the length, width, and height of the ark, it says nothing about the dimensions of the door. That this detail is missing doesn't seem accidental. It suggests that in Christ there is unlimited access to eternal salvation.[6] All may enter into safety regardless of the height or depth of their sins. The grace of salvation symbolized in this metaphor of the Bible's first book is stated explicitly in the Bible's last book, in one of my favorite texts: "The Spirit and the bride say, Come. And let him that heareth say, Come. And let him that is athirst come. And whosoever will, let him take the water of life freely" (Revelation 22:17, KJV).

"Then the LORD said to Noah, 'Go into the ark, you and your whole family' " (Genesis 7:1). It isn't enough to know there is a door; we have to enter through it in order to be saved. We can admire the ark, visit the ark, speak well of it to others, and invite them to go in, but we aren't saved until we enter ourselves. We must go inside of the ark because that is where God resides. It wasn't the type of wood Noah used or the engineering secrets he employed that made the ark a saving vessel. The presence and power of God were the only guarantees of salvation even in this divinely designed ship. Three stories high with one door and no lifeboats, it was the symbol of complete trust in God.

Furthermore, the ark of Noah had no sails, no oars, no engine, and no rudder—no way for the passengers to take things out of God's hands and into their own. The ark had a Captain but no co-captain. Everyone on board was a passenger. To come into the ark was to trust entirely in God. In the same way, Jesus Christ is the Captain of our souls and the only guarantee of salvation from sin and death. He is the Door and He is the Ark itself. We not only enter through Him, that is through the gift of His Spirit within, but we also live and grow in sanctification as we abide in Him and put our trust in Him through the obedience of faith. It is His presence that gives confidence and certainty to our lives so that we don't have to live in fear even in an unfriendly and dangerous world.

THE ARK OF SALVATION

On the night of the storm on the Sea of Galilee, the disciples would have enjoyed their trip more had they remembered Noah's ark (Matthew 8:23, 24). The sudden, furious tempest took them by surprise even though some of them were fishermen who surely must have survived storms on this sea before. This time, however, they were overwhelmed. It wasn't till they had gone from fear to panic that they remembered Jesus was on board and that He was the One who bade them cross the sea in the first place. So when Jesus awoke to the frantic cries, "Lord, save us! We're going to drown!" He rebuked them mildly, saying, "You of little faith, why are you so afraid?" Their fear revealed the weakness of their faith. The disciples should have known by now that any vessel Jesus boards immediately becomes unsinkable. But even though their faith was weak, Jesus didn't desert them. He chastised them, but He still saved them, showing once again that salvation comes solely by grace.

Noah was perfect in his generation, but that is not what saved him. Instead, "Noah found grace in the eyes of the LORD" (Genesis 6:8). This is the first occurrence of the word *grace* in Scripture. Noah found grace, but this gift required a vehicle, so God commanded the construction of the ark, which would be the place of safety until the storm was over. And when it was over, God gave the sign that represented His covenant: the rainbow in the clouds.

Noah's ark was a big boat made of cypress wood; baby Moses' "ark" was a basket floating in the reeds; and Israel's ark was the sacred chest that contained the tables of stone the Israelites carried through the wilderness. And different as they were from each other, all of them were, in one sense or another, arks of the covenant.

Scripture gives us just a cursory description of Noah's ark, but it goes into a lot of detail about the sanctuary in the wilderness. Five chapters of Exodus are devoted to laying out its dimensions and furnishings. There are similarities between Noah's ark and the sanctuary. For instance, Noah's ark had three decks, each of which, according to the measurements, was the same height as the sanctuary.[7]

Noah's ark was a place of safety—a refuge where its passengers could ride out the storm. But it wasn't really the ark that saved those within it; they were saved by the God who commanded the building of the ark and who watched over it throughout the great storms that cleansed the earth. Noah and his family were saved as they rested in faith in Jesus.

In a sense, then, Jesus Himself is the final, most effective Ark. Those who find refuge in this Ark of the Covenant of God, who put their trust in Him, will live eternally. He is our ultimate Refuge from the storm, and He will not fail us.

THE FAMILY MAN

For 120 years Noah preached repentance as he built the only means of salvation from the destruction that was coming. There were those who heeded the warning and joined the ark project but who died before the Flood came. The majority, though, never were converted. Because most people ignored Noah's message, we tend to think of him as a great shipbuilder but a weak evangelist. The Bible, however, presents another perspective. "By faith Noah, being warned about things not yet seen, moved in holy fear and built an ark *to save his family*" (Hebrews 11:7; emphasis added).

For nine hundred years, the world's first man saw his offspring come into the world, and he was able to repeat to his grandchildren and to his great-greats the story of the Fall and then the expulsion from the Garden. What an impression his story must have made on all who heard it!

It was hard to deny the authority of God while Adam was still alive, but with his death wickedness lost its last natural restraint and went on a violent rampage. This was the world of Noah, a world in which Satan had almost accomplished his purpose of securing the entire human family for his kingdom. If there was one thing more astounding than the sin of Noah's age, it was the miracle that out of it God could still save human beings.

Noah's life offers lessons that can be a blessing to us all. Genesis says, "Noah was a righteous man, blameless among the people of his time, and he walked with God. Noah had three sons: Shem, Ham, and Japheth" (Genesis 6:9, 10, NIV).

Noah walked with God, and he was blameless. These two ideas are inseparable. Noah was blameless in his generation. He took no part in the high-handed iniquity of his day, but instead took a stand against it. He didn't cheat his neighbors or flirt with their wives; he was upright and honest, and his sons saw it. They watched him as they were growing up, and they knew they had a father who was genuine. Noah was an example to his boys; the influence of his life made a deep impression on them.

This is an example of the contribution to child development parents make, often without even realizing it. The strongest asset parents have is their example. It means something to have a parent you can look up to, one who won't compromise or take part in sin. It sets for the child an internal standard he can never escape even if at first he doesn't live up to it. His conscience will continually tell him what he should be: "Train up a child in the way he should go, and when he is old he will not depart from it" (Proverbs 22:6, NKJV).

INSEPARABLE

The two things said of Noah in Genesis 6:9 are intimately related. The only way to be blameless is to walk with God. To walk with God means to abide in Him at all times, whatever our circumstances. It means, in the words of Paul, to bring "every thought into captivity to the obedience of Christ" (2 Corinthians 10:5, NKJV). This is the goal of sanctification.

In the three phrases used to describe Noah's righteousness, commentators see a progression in his spiritual growth. First, Scripture says that "he was a righteous man"; then that "he was blameless in his time"; and finally, that "he walked with God."[8] Noah grew in the life of righteousness, just as Enoch had. He shunned evil through "a determined recognition of God."[9] He consciously made God his choice until, through consistently strengthening the relationship, exercising it became a habit. Noah worked at seeing everything from God's perspective until God's view became his view. This was his experience of walking with God.

In describing Noah's experience, Hebrews classifies his righteousness as belonging to the category of faith,[10] and this is critical since faith is the only category to which saving righteousness can be attributed. There are other kinds of righteousness, but no way to be saved other than through *righteousness by faith.* Here is a challenge to the religion that says self-discipline produces righteousness. Self-discipline may enable some people to maintain a strict outward conformity to biblical standards, but faith in God is the only source of salvation; otherwise, the motivation to obey might originate in selfishness, which would make that "obedience" of no more worth than was the self-centered rebellion of Lamech. Obedience may be born of motives other than the glory of God. People may obey in order to maintain their image or standing in the community. They may obey because of pride, like the Pharisees, or even because of fear. But only the obedience of faith in God results in salvation. Noah's obedience wouldn't have stood the test of the rejection and ridicule of the world had it not been rooted in his love for and faith in God.

For 120 years Noah never wavered from God's mission for his life. Babies were born, grew up, became adults, got married, had babies of their own, and those babies grew up and had babies of *their* own, and Noah was still building. It was a project that called for great faith and required all of his gifts—the architectural ingenuity to plot God's in-structions, the physical brawn to prepare and place the construction materials, the commitment to keep at it day and night, and even his wealth. Noah invested his own money in the ark project until he had none left.[11]

Noah gave the job his all. That's what it takes to save a family today too: *everything*. We must be totally sold on the task. As fathers and mothers, whether raising a family with or without a spouse, we must be true to God inside and out because we cannot give to our families something we do not ourselves possess. And we cannot fake commit-ment. Children will forgive our shortcomings and mistakes—all par-ents make them; but they will not forgive hypocrisy. They will notice when we put on one face for the church and another for the world, and they will resent us. They will rebel against God just to get back at us. It takes everything to serve God and save your family, to walk with God and shun the evil of the world.

"Noah was six hundred years old when the floodwaters came on the earth. And Noah and his sons and his wife and his sons' wives entered the ark to escape the waters of the flood" (Genesis 7:6, 7). When we calculate the ages of Noah's sons, we realize that he started to build the ark before his sons were born. When they came into the world, their father was already doing the work that would save their lives. Shem, Ham, and Japheth grew up with the ark. They worked on it themselves from the time they were old enough to hold a hammer.

Don't wait to become a parent before you start to serve God. Get started now. Become the person you want your children to be, be-cause it is certain that they will imitate you. Here's a promise that believing parents love to claim: "Thus says the LORD: 'Even the cap-tives of the mighty shall be taken away, and the prey of the terrible be delivered; for I will contend with him who contends with you. *And I will save your children'* " (Isaiah 49:25, NKJV; emphasis added). This is a beautiful promise. We can always count on God to keep His word, but we must note that this promise has conditions. It is hypocritical for us to ask God to save our children when we're not willing to participate ourselves. Here's God's word through Jeremiah: "Obey me, and I will be your God and you will be my people. Walk in all the ways I command you, *that it may go well with you*" (Jeremiah 7:23; emphasis added).

With these words we have come full circle: Walk with God and obey His commands, completely shunning evil. Do not wait till you become a parent to make this commitment; start now. If you do so, God will save your family.

WHEN DISASTER STRIKES

The rain began on the seventeenth day of the second month, and it didn't stop for forty days. Water poured down from above, and it erupted from beneath the earth. Aquifers exploded with volcanic force, catapulting great boulders hundreds of feet into the air—boulders so large and heavy that they shook the earth when they landed. The people who had mocked Noah and called him a fool weren't laughing anymore. They knocked on the door of the ark, but Noah couldn't open it. Judgment Day had come. In fact, things get so brutal that Satan himself feared for his life. He also thought Judgment Day had come and that God was going to do him in right then.

Hurricane Camille (1969) was one of the worst storms ever to make landfall in the United States. With wind speeds of 190 miles per hour, Camille devastated the coast of Mississippi, taking 259 lives along the way. We'll never know how strong it was at its peak because it destroyed all of the instruments that recorded the speed of its winds.[12]

Despite the threat Hurricane Camille posed, a group of residents on the Mississippi Gulf coast refused to evacuate their homes. They decided instead to hold a "hurricane party," though their apartment was just 250 feet from the water's edge and directly in the line of danger.

The local chief of police got wind of the planned festivities and paid the prospective partiers a visit. The tide was already rising and the winds were beginning to pick up when he arrived at the apartment complex. Seeing a man on a second-floor balcony with a drink in his hand, the chief yelled to him, "You need to clear out!"

The man replied, "This is my property, and you'll have to arrest me to get me off of it."

The chief tried to persuade others to leave, but he had no success. So, as a last-ditch effort to convey the danger they were taking on, he asked them for the names of their next of kin. As they told him the names, they laughed him to scorn.

At 10:15 P.M. the front wall of the storm came ashore. Raindrops hit with the force of bullets, and the incoming waves crested between twenty-two and twenty-eight feet high. And when the storm was over, it was reported that the worst damage had occurred at the complex where the partygoers had refused the chief's warning. Nothing was left of the three-story structure, and the only survivor was a five-year-old boy found clinging to a mattress. The people in this complex had ample time to reach safety. But like the antediluvians of Noah's time, they ignored the warnings they received, and they suffered the consequences.

There are lessons in this story for those who live in the end time. Jesus tied the story of Noah and his ark to His prophecy of the Second Coming: "As it was in the days of Noah, so it will be at the coming of the Son of Man" (Matthew 24:37).

These are the days of which Jesus spoke, and we are called to come into the Ark of safety, which is Jesus Christ Himself.

OBEDIENCE: ABRAHAM
CHAPTER 6

Abram left, as the LORD had told him.
—Genesis 12:4

In the early 1950s, the British Broadcasting Corporation (BBC) sent a film crew to the South Pacific. They were to report on an unusual ritual carried out by the men of Pentecost Island, one of eighty-three islands that make up the Republic of Vanuatu. Pentecost is a "throwback" island, a land frozen in time, with no cities or towns and nothing in the way of what we would call entertainment. The villagers grow their own food and continue to follow many ancient customs and rituals. Tourists pay large sums of money to see the men of Pentecost practice the *nanghol,* a ceremonial rite of passage that signifies acceptance into manhood.

As the BBC reporters watched, a young man scaled a hundred-foot-tall tower made of saplings and branches tied together with vines. Stone-faced and still, he paused dramatically and drew in a deep breath or two. Then, with a look of determination, he launched himself into the air headfirst, his body stiff and straight as an arrow, his pupils dilated, his arms folded across his chest. The onlookers gasped as he plummeted downward at sixty miles per hour, heading for certain death—until a vine attached to his ankles went taut and stopped his descent with a jerk just as the top of his head grazed the ground. When he stopped swinging, he walked away from that tower as a new man who had just been born into the community.

There is an analogy here to the leap of faith that launches the believer into covenant relationship with God. In no life is it exemplified better than in the life of the patriarch Abraham.

THE FRIEND OF GOD

Abraham is, arguably, the most outstanding figure in salvation history other than Jesus Himself. The story of Abraham occupies fourteen chapters in the book of Genesis; his name is mentioned in twenty-six other Bible books, including all four Gospels; and in three places in Scripture he bears the intimate title "the friend of God" (2 Chronicles 20:7; Isaiah 41:8; James 2:23). In fact, this title serves as a moniker for Abraham, a sort of nickname, and it brings to mind a question that is of interest to every believer, *How does one become a friend of God? What process must one go through?*

As we read Abraham's life story, we discover that he wasn't an outstanding person by the usual measures of greatness. He performed no miracles, built no city, wrote no theology nor any books that we know of. He didn't invent anything, create anything, discover anything, or name anything. He didn't produce a great philosophy or cure a deadly disease or die as a martyr for a great cause. Abraham did none of the things to which we usually attribute renown, and so we wonder why God considered him to be so outstanding.

The story of this outstanding man begins in Genesis 12: "The LORD had said to Abram, 'Leave your country . . . and go to the land I will show you. I will make you into a great nation and I will bless you' " (Genesis 12:1, 2). After the Fall in the Garden of Eden, humanity took a careening spiral downward further and further away from God. The shocking homicide in the first family was followed by one atrocity after another until by the time of Noah, things were as bad as they could possibly get.

Humanity's wretchedness brought grief to the heart of God. To protect the descendants of Seth, the reign of sin had to be checked. God had no choice but to destroy the world and start again, which explains the Flood. In His mercy, God didn't destroy *all* humankind and create a brand-new world. Instead, He gave humanity a second chance through Ham, Shem, and Japheth; He wanted them to produce more Enochs and Noahs and no more Cains.

God also unveiled a new strategy. He wouldn't send a new philosophy to be studied, an advanced theorem to be researched, a new set of propositions to be mastered. Instead, He would reveal Himself through a special relationship with one man and his descendants, thus demonstrating to all humankind what it means to live the life of faith and obedience to God.

God looked over the whole earth in search of a subject for His great project, and then He chose a man who had been following his father on a pilgrimage that never reached its intended destination. Terah and his family, who were from Ur, got stuck while on the way to Canaan when one of Terah's sons died in Haran. After Terah died, too, God looked on the remaining son and decided He would bless him and through him demonstrate to all people what life can be like when you have the right Friend. So, God called Abraham.

Right away we notice the primary feature of the covenant God made with Abraham: it began one-sidedly. Before Abraham did anything, before he came to know God or had heard anything about God's covenant, God discovered him. The first step toward becoming God's friend, then, is the divine initiative. Abraham didn't seek God; it was God who sought Abraham, wanting to start a relationship with him that was entirely a divine idea and was to be implemented for a divine purpose.

That is a continuing truth. Jeremiah wrote that when God called him, He said, "Before I formed you in the womb I knew you, before you were born I set you apart; I appointed you as a prophet to the nations" (Jeremiah 1:5). And Jesus told His disciples, "You did not choose me, but I chose you and appointed you to go and bear fruit—fruit that will last" (John 15:16).

When the Lord God came to Abraham, who was living in Haran with what was left of his father's family, He made a covenant with him when Abraham didn't know what a covenant was. The Lord made a promise to Abraham that changed his life. Abraham wasn't expecting it, nor did it come because he had earned it. It was completely God's initiative, based not on Abraham's merit but on God's sovereign choice.

GOD'S GLORY
Every journey with God begins in the same way—the Lord starts

pursuing us long before we have begun to think of Him. In fact, we would never seek God at all if He didn't seek us first. Friendship with God is always initiated from the divine side. Our coming to God is a response to His coming to us, and, in fact, we couldn't come to Him were it not for the grace that enables us to make the decision of faith (Romans 8:6). While we are out in the world, competing in the marketplace, pursuing our earthly dreams, seeking admiration, wading blindly into and out of illegitimate relationships, creating our own brand of "freedom," God was thinking of us. He was sending us messages of invitation through life experiences, good and bad. He was speaking to us through His servants—known to us and unknown—giving us flashes of His light through people of grace He brings into our lives. And He was watching over us through the ministry of holy angels in order to keep us from drifting too far away from Him. God was thinking of us and acting for our salvation when we weren't thinking of Him. Scripture goes so far as to say that we were chosen by God in Christ even before we came into existence (Ephesians 1:4). That's divine initiative, and it's the only way God's covenant comes to us.

God's divine initiative has implications for the plan of redemption as well. In our condition of helplessness and need, it is easy for us to think that the plan of redemption was created solely for us, for our salvation. But divine initiative suggests something else. God established the plan of redemption by which we are saved to project His own glory throughout the universe. The primary goal of the plan of redemption is to vindicate God, the One "for whom and through whom everything exists"; "for from him and through him and to him are all things" (Hebrews 2:10; Romans 11:36).

The sovereignty of God means that the universe is His—He owns it. Through false accusations, Lucifer planted seeds of doubt about the Almighty. That started a rebellion in heaven that led to all-out war. When that war spread to earth, God activated His reserve plan. In His mercy, He didn't condemn the fallen of earth to the same fate as the fallen angels of heaven, whom the Bible says are now being held for judgment and then will suffer eternal fire (Matthew 25:41; 2 Peter 2:4). God decided instead to pay, through the death of His Son, the ransom for humanity's sin and in this way reveal to the angels and to the unfallen worlds His true character of love. The plan of salvation was formed to bring the whole of creation, including the universe's one fallen world, back to oneness and wholeness.

The sacrifice of Jesus brought it all about. His decision to identify Himself with humanity by becoming one of us brought the attention of the entire universe to this planet. Scripture says of Jesus:

> He is the image of the invisible God, the firstborn over all creation. For by him all things were created: things in heaven and on earth, visible and invisible, whether thrones or powers or rulers or authorities; all things were created by him and for him . . . so that in everything he might have the supremacy (Colossians 1:15–18).

If it is a blow to our ego to discover that neither creation nor redemption was principally crafted for our glory, it is only because we judge the matter from the standpoint of our humanity. Whenever spiritual truth is judged carnally—that is, according to the flesh—we come to wrong conclusions. We would even feel tempted to use one of *our* words to describe the divine motive in redemption, a word that has no place in heaven nor anywhere else in the universe but on earth; a word that belongs completely and only to us: *selfish*. That God should enact the plan of redemption not primarily for the lost but for Himself rubs us the wrong way. When we think it through, though, we realize that the very assumption on our part that God could do anything selfishly springs from our sinful nature. Not even the perfect pair of the Garden of Eden, creatures made in the image of God, could perform a single act out of selfishness, because it had no place in the human heart until they sinned. But those who haven't been regenerated view everything through their corrupted natures and feel offended at not being the center of attention in the plan of redemption. Without regeneration, it would never occur to us that the great sacrifice God made in giving the gift of His Son at the highest possible cost to Himself could be for a purpose even greater than our rescue. It would never occur to us that the universe couldn't be healed by our ransom alone but only through the vindication of God in which the unique role of the redeemed is to be the undeniable evidence of His glory. While our glory has no power to bless anyone but ourselves, the whole universe is uplifted whenever God is glorified. The ultimate reward of the saved of earth, even beyond receiving new robes and a crown, is to see Jesus exalted to the highest place and God glorified without a rival by every creature in heaven, in earth, and under the earth (Philippians 2:9–11).

FAITH AND WORKS

When God called and made covenant promises, Abraham had to respond. And the only appropriate response to God's invitation is consent—but not with mere intellectual consent. No, the consent that saves based on faith reveals itself in the form of obedience, and unquestioning obedience at that. This is always the result of true faith in God and is the only saving response to the divinely initiated offer of covenant. God's invitation is also a claim based on His creatorship, and when we realize this truth, we respond as Abraham did. This is the second step in becoming a friend of God—the human response of obedience to God.

In order to know the intimacy God longs to share with us, we must take God at His word and obey everything He says. The downfall of humankind began in the Garden with unbelief and disobedience; conversely, the redemption of humanity begins with faith and obedience. We cannot receive salvation until we believe and obey, and not even God will force our obedience. Without our consent in the form of active faith, the greatest power in the universe—the power of divine love expressed in grace—is wasted on us. Faith stalls and peters out when we don't comply with God's will. This is not works-righteousness but the natural outcome of belief in the God who not only gives His love but also gives His requirements.

Divine love comes with a claim, and truly accepting God's love means living up to His expectations empowered by His grace. This distinction between works as the companion of faith and works in the place of faith is clearly set forth in Scripture. It is a distinction that sometimes is misunderstood when the writings of Paul and James— both of whom use Abraham as their paradigm—are interpreted as being in conflict with each other. Here's what Paul wrote: "The promise to Abraham or to his descendants that he would be heir of the world was not through the Law." "We maintain that a man is *justified by faith apart from works* of the Law" (Romans 4:13; 3:28, NASB; emphasis added). And here are James's words: "Was not Abraham our father *justified by works* when he offered up Isaac his son on the altar?" (James 2:21, 22, NASB; emphasis added).

Read superficially, the statements appear to be in complete contradiction, Paul making a claim for justification without works and James arguing for justification by works. But the two apostles were writing from different perspectives and with differing emphases. Paul was refuting the idea that good works can in any way secure salvation. James, on the other hand, was showing the necessary connection between saving faith and its fruit, good works. Both writers had the same thing in mind when they spoke of "works"; they even used the same word. But the application is different for each. They were teaching two compatible truths, both of which apply to Abraham without contradiction. James, who pictured faith as action, is not at odds with Paul, who was teaching faith's role in justification. Paul was explaining that we can't allow works to get out of its place and attempt to replace faith, while James was teaching that works, in their proper place, serve to confirm faith. To be saved, we cannot be looking to our works. But when we're in Christ, our salvation must bear fruit in works like His (see John 15). While faith in Christ is the only means of salvation, works for and by Christ are the only true evidence of salvation, and Abraham possessed them both. "You see that his faith and his actions were working together, and his faith was made complete by what he did" (James 2:22, 23).

So, Abraham collected all of his family and all of his possessions and set out for the place where God had told him to go. And when his friends asked him where he was going, he couldn't answer. He couldn't supply a practical, logical, or rational explanation for what he was doing—not yet anyway. God might make His plan clearer to him at some future time, but for now, all Abraham knew was that he had to obey God's command. Abraham was exercising a kind of obedience that has almost completely lost its place in our culture today, obedience without knowing and without question. "By faith Abraham, when called to go to a place he would later receive as his inheritance, obeyed and went, *even though he did not know* where he was going" (Hebrews 11:8, 9; emphasis added).

The going-without-knowing is what bothers us. That intelligent beings should be asked to do anything without question offends our sense of liberty. It contradicts postmodern culture's emphasis on individual rights. At the very least, it's an archaic concept that fits previous generations better than it does ours, sounding more like something out of the fourteenth century than out of the twenty-first. It belongs to the days of serfs and nobles, when privilege and servitude were birthrights passed down from one generation to the next; when English vocabulary included words like *holpen* and *whithersoever* and children bowed to their parents and wives called their husbands "my lord." We don't say *whithersoever* anymore, and children no longer bow to their parents. And as for what wives call their husbands these days, well, perhaps we had better leave that alone. I think we can agree, however, that it is not "my lord."

What then are we talking about here? Is there yet a place in the life of the believer for unquestioning obedience? I say there is. I know what I'm arguing for is a rare thing, but I do argue for it. There is room in the life of the Christ follower for unquestioning obedience. There is still a single relationship to which it pertains. And I would like to take us to the insignificant experience of an obscure Bible character to illustrate the point.

AN EXAMPLE

"When the boy had almost reached the arrow, Jonathan shouted, 'The arrow is still ahead of you. Hurry, hurry, don't wait.' So the boy quickly gathered up the arrows and ran back to his master. He, of course, suspected nothing; only Jonathan and David understood the signal" (1 Samuel 20:37–39, NLT).

The context of this incident is the mission of Jonathan, the prince, to save David from the murderous intent of King Saul, the prince's father. The retrieving of the arrows had a secret meaning: Jonathan's directions to the servant boy were in a code that would tell David whether or not it was safe for him to appear at the palace. While the servant boy was picking up the arrows, David was in hiding, interpreting Jonathan's cryptic message. It told him that all was not safe—he must run for his life.

Secrecy was indispensable to the success of this venture. If Jonathan had found it necessary to explain himself in order to get his servant to do what was required, the entire plan would have been placed in jeopardy. But the servant boy was accustomed to obeying commands without question, and because of this, he became the instrument of a purpose that was higher than he knew. He thought he was just recovering arrows, while in fact he was saving the life of Israel's next king—one who would be a progenitor of the Messiah! In other words, he was preserving the royal line and assisting God's plan of salvation. It was the servant's willingness to serve without distinction and obey without question that made him useful. And to this day there is heroism in simple obedience to the commands of God that is based on blind faith.

In the military, a command from a superior officer needs no reason other than the will of the commander; in that sense it is arbitrary. Disobeying such a command would result in consequences of the most undesirable kind for the offending soldier, including possible court martial. But outside of the military this kind of compliance doesn't exist anymore, not even in our relationship with God. Unquestioning obedience appears not to apply in what we call free societies. The only kind of obeying that is required today is obeying one's own ambitions. This has become the new standard of integrity. Keeping faith with oneself takes priority over keeping faith with recognized authority—the family, the state, the church, the Creator.

Don't "settle"?

In a recent episode of *So You Think You Can Dance*—one of the many "reality" shows that now dominate TV programming—the judges asked a contestant who barely missed the final cut if she intended to audition again the following year. When she answered that this had been her last shot and that she would now move on to other things, she was castigated for the great crime of "giving up on her dreams." The judges reacted with horror that at so early an age a young woman should make a practical decision and "settle" for going back to school. It apparently didn't occur to them that she might be driven by a sense of duty more important than a dream. It seemed out of the question to even consider whether she might be better suited for some other venture that was worthy of her efforts. Personal ambition was the religion of the highest order, and to accept limitation—the one undeniable reality that applies to all finite creatures—was considered to be a sin of the most egregious kind. The only thing that mattered was the idolatry of believing in oneself.

The experience of this embarrassed young woman demonstrates what has become so pervasive a cultural value as to be the centerpiece of popular Christianity. Some of the most prominent Christian ministers of today preach this false gospel: "God has a big dream for your life"; "God sees you as a champion. He believes in you even more than you believe in yourself"; "God has confidence in you."[1] "Because I was taught to believe in myself, I am now doing things that were once just little dream seeds in my mind. . . . Many people with my background would not have attempted such pursuits, but I did—because I believed in myself."[2]

The new meaning of Christian faith is that God believes in you, and your dreams define His will for your life. Divine love means God values your earthly desires, and if your faith is strong enough, He will indulge you by fulfilling them. So, the glory of the Creator is turned into the glory of the creature, whose material success becomes the proof that Christian faith is valid and worthwhile. And if you don't receive the raise or promotion you prayed for, if you still can't afford to buy your dream house or dream car, this is not a sign that God has other, more important priorities for your life. It's a sign that your faith is weak—you haven't prayed enough, believed in yourself enough, or perhaps not given enough to the church. The obedience of faith is not that you should comply with what God requires of you, but that He will comply with what you require of Him. When this misguided teaching becomes the focus of the believer's life, the attainment of spiritual excellence is derailed and the ambition to attain the beauty of the character of Christ is lost sight of.

Rick Warren calls believers of this kind "worldly Christians." "Worldly Christians," he says, "look to God primarily for personal fulfillment. . . . Their prayers focus on their own needs, blessings, and happiness. It's a 'me-first' faith: How can God make *my* life more comfortable? They want to use God for their purposes instead of *being* used for *his* purposes."[3]

What Scripture says on this subject is clear; it decidedly contradicts the popular theology. The highest faith is not that we should believe in ourselves but that we should believe in Christ with all of our hearts. Faith begins with the acceptance of the fact that we don't know what will make us truly happy or what we really need. Faith means believing that since Jesus has the eternal view while we are limited to the temporal view, He knows better than we do what is for our good. Faith is proven as we by grace submit to God's dreams for our lives, not as we ask Him to submit to our dreams for ourselves. Said the psalmist, "I delight to do *your will*, O my God, and *your law* is within my heart" (Psalm 40:8, NKJV; emphasis added). And Jesus expressed the central theme of His life in these words: "I seek not to please myself but him who sent me" (John 5:30).

This life principle—"not my will but thine, O Lord"—was modeled to the highest degree in the life of Abraham. His faith was revealed by his unquestioning obedience, which was the ultimate proof of his loyalty to God. Indeed, one could argue that the kind of obedience that is generated by faith reached its pinnacle in Abraham, in that he obeyed to the point of placing himself and his family at risk, following even though he "did not know where he was going" (Hebrews 11:8). His faith was most complete when he had no sight. He chose to believe without a reason, not based on his dream for himself but on God's dream for him even though he didn't fully understand God's dream. It was faith as humble submission rather than self-exalting ambition. The first represents God's highest ideal for His followers, while the second leads to the ruin of our God-given gifts and talents, a ruin that not even the wisest of us can avert. The example of Solomon substantiates these conclusions:

> Almost imperceptibly he [Solomon] began to trust less and less in divine guidance and blessing, and to put confidence in his own strength. . . . An ambition to excel all other nations in power and grandeur led him to pervert for selfish purposes the heavenly gifts hitherto employed for the glory of God.[4]

HUMAN SOVEREIGNTY

Choice is the human form of sovereignty, but compared to divine sovereignty, human sovereignty is a mere analogy. Human freedom always has limits, while divine freedom has none. Choice functions in the life of the believer as it has since the Garden of Eden—it serves as the test of faith. It is the pivot enabling people to choose between obedience and disobedience; to choose whether we will take the fruit for ourselves or submit to God's unexplained command. As we consider the choice, we can hear the serpent in the forbidden tree as he tries to seduce us to reach for the highest goal of personal ambition and self-love by offering the age-old inducement, "You will be like God." "Whenever pride and ambition are indulged, the life is marred, for pride, feeling no need, closes the heart against the infinite blessings of Heaven. He who makes self-glorification his aim will find himself destitute of the grace of God."[5]

When God initiates His call to us, He never tries to motivate us by telling us how good we can have it here—even though the life of faith is the best, most fruitful, and most joyful life we can know. It *is* the best life we can live now. But this world is passing away, and God has plans for us that are eternal. This life is preparation for the next, and like Abraham, the friend of God never loses sight of this.

The call of God is a call to partnership bound by an unbreakable bond of faith and love. In their heart of hearts, all believers know this. But here is the part many Christians do not realize because popular Christianity has obscured it: Friendship with God is always on God's terms, not on ours. Friendship with God is not a democratic arrangement that makes us equal partners with God. We don't get to choose the course of our journey on the path of faith. God calls us to oneness with Himself not to fulfill our will but so that His will might be fulfilled in us, and just like Abraham, we don't know what that means. God's ways are mysterious to us. We couldn't fully understand them even if He were to stand visibly before us and explain them to us directly. We have to walk blindly at times, not knowing the way but knowing the One who knows the way. God calls us to trust Him. He knows what He is doing in our lives even when we cannot see what He's directing us toward, and He won't water down His Word to make it easier for us to accept. It is what it is. So the question becomes, do you trust God? Do you trust Him with your life, with the lives of your children, and with everything else that is dear to you?

Oswald Chambers made these profound statements about the obedience of faith:

> The natural man insists on explanations, because whatever he can explain, he can command. In the spiritual domain nothing is explained until we obey, and then it is not so much an explanation as an instant discernment. . . .
>
> Only [up]on looking back over the path of obedience do we realize what God's idea has been all along, for God sanctifies memory.[6]

A PERSON, NOT A PLACE

In the beginning, Abraham thought God was taking him on a journey to a place. That was all he could understand at the time. By the end, Abraham saw what all the patriarchs and prophets eventually learned, that all along God was leading him on an odyssey to a Person, and He was that Person. Saving faith is founded on knowing a Person, not knowing a theology, an ideology, or a doctrine.

There is a sense, in fact, in which the duties we undertake in obedience to God are never completed in this life. Abraham never owned the land he was sent to inhabit. The promise was fulfilled, but he didn't see the fulfillment. The same pattern repeats itself again and again in the lives of Bible characters. Moses never entered the Promised Land that he fought so hard to bring his people to. John the Baptist was beheaded by the potentate whose sinful life he had condemned in the name of the Lord. Paul was executed by Nero, the enemy of the church the apostle had worked so assiduously to build up. Peter was crucified upside down. Even Jesus, the Captain of salvation, ended His mission in apparent defeat, nailed to a tree in shame, ridiculed by His enemies as He hung covered in blood and gasping for breath. The work we undertake in the name of Jesus will be accomplished—but not in this life. In this age, kingdom work is always unfinished business.

What's the point then? Why go to the trouble, put up with the abuse, struggle against the tide, if our efforts are doomed to fail anyway? Abraham, the father of the faithful, had the answer. Paul said Abraham "was looking forward to the city with foundations, whose architect and builder is God" (Hebrews 11:10).

Abraham wasn't so concerned with the Promised Land of this age; he knew it would eventually pass away. Abraham was looking for the Promised Land constructed by God that will last forever. For Abraham, faith and obedience meant living *in* the present but not *for* the present. Abraham was living in the here and now, but doing so with his eye on the future. The friend of God wasn't concerned with how much he could accumulate in this life. He wanted the *heavenly* mansion, the *heavenly* kingdom; and more than that, he wanted the heavenly King. "So we fix our eyes not on what is seen, but on what is unseen. For what is seen is temporary, but what is unseen is eternal" (2 Corinthians 4:18).

Here is the crux of the matter; God cannot have His way in our lives if we have Him boxed in. We must love and trust God enough to obey what He's commanded in His Word without further explanation if it comes to that—and it will come to that.

Do you want to be a friend of God? Study the life of Abraham. Friendship with God consists of the divine initiative in calling, the human response in the obedience of faith-without-sight, and the complete sacrifice of self-surrender, holding nothing back.

At the 2004 General Conference year-end meetings, people were talking about the oldest living Seventh-day Adventist, Lydia Newton. When she was born, Oklahoma was still a territory and the average life span in the United States was forty-six years. The first-ever World Series was played when she was ten years old, a best-of-nine format won by the Boston Americans. Mother's Day was created when she was twenty-one.

When Lydia's family doctor died of old age and her new physician got her chart, he referred her to a pediatrician—he thought the birth date '93 meant 1993. In Lydia's senior years, her daughter and son-in-law took care of her. They were eighty-nine when she moved in with them. Lydia Newton herself was 112 years old when she died!

There's something to be said about a lifetime with God that stretches through the years. One doesn't reach one hundred years of living as a disciple of Jesus without trials, suffering, and tests of one's faith. But here's the final reward of faith in Christ: it isn't bigger houses or more luxurious cars; it is the eternity it purchases in the promise of redemption that cannot fail. When faith becomes sight, 112 years will seem like a minute, and the redeemed one will see that the entire journey of life on earth was just the starting gate for an eternity-long relationship with the Redeemer.

JUDGMENT: SODOM
CHAPTER 7

"I have given her time to repent of her immorality, but she is unwilling."
—*Revelation 2:21*

The human heart is a marvelous organ. This life pump sustains the body by circulating blood to every organ, thus supplying the vital materials the body needs and removing the waste. Only the size of a fist and weighing a mere ten ounces at maturity, the heart does an amazing amount of work. It begins to beat prenatally, about twenty-one days after conception, and doesn't cease until the day we die—in an average lifetime, 2.5 billion beats later. And all of its work is involuntary; we aren't conscious of what it's doing, yet it is always at work.

We can find analogies to the spiritual life in the heart. In Scripture, the word *heart* is used of the authentic person, the person we really are inwardly. The heart is the place of decisive spiritual activity, the place of communion with God. Its operation is hidden and mysterious to us; no science can discover it. "The heart," said French writer Blaise Pascal, "has its reasons of which reason knows nothing."

The story of Lot and his family reveals this truth from the negative side. It is a story of warnings, of consequences, and of the mysterious, paradoxical workings of God's wrath from a divine heart that is all love.

SODOMITES
"The two men said to Lot, 'Do you have anyone else here—sons-in-law, sons or daughters, or anyone else in the city who belongs

113

to you? Get them out of here, because we are going to destroy this place' " (Genesis 19:12, 13).

The biblical story of Sodom and Gomorrah draws back the curtain between the spiritual and natural realms and reveals secrets we don't usually see. Holy angels are always among us, constantly contending with demons and fallen human beings in order to lead as many as possible to God and to keep God's people safe in an alien and hostile world. Citizens of the kingdom of heaven who live as strangers in the realm of sin wouldn't last a single day were it not for the tireless ministry of this celestial Secret Service. The angels are most active when the controversy between good and evil is most stark, and in the case of Sodom they were sent to protect the one remaining family that could still be saved.

The incident at Lot's house shows how completely corrupt beyond redemption the citizens of Sodom had become. Even the most sensitive person can see how necessary, even essential, was the judgment of God in this case. The hearts of the Sodomites had become callous beyond repair. Their every deed and their influence served only to advance evil, and their continued existence was a constant threat to God's people and an affront to the loving heart of the lofty One whose name is Holy (Isaiah 57:15).

When it comes to Lot's wife, however, we aren't so sure. She had been chosen to be saved and had escaped the conflagration. How then could she be doomed to suffer the same fate as the wicked for merely looking back? She'd just left her married daughters and their husbands behind to perish, so surely her concern is understandable. Why such a harsh judgment? All she did was turn her head, and it cost her life. Is that how easy it is to be lost?

When I was a child, these questions troubled me. In my immaturity, I couldn't understand how a simple bodily movement could result in such tragedy. But when we look deeply into the story with the eyes of an adult, not a child, we see a meaning beyond outward behavior that is most relevant—an inner meaning that reveals the corruption in the heart of Lot's wife due to the evil affects of too much wealth and too much leisure.

THE EFFECT OF LUXURY

Sodom and Gomorrah were beautiful cities, the most beautiful in the Jordan Valley. Luxuriant vegetation, tropical fruit, flowers that blossomed year round—it was the Garden of Eden reborn. The abundance of the land led to ease of life and the hoarding of wealth, and this became the city's downfall.[1] Gardens and vineyards and costly mansions were in abundant supply, and too much luxury led to idleness and selfishness, which opened the door to a thousand temptations.

"Behold, this was the guilt of your sister Sodom: she and her daughters had arrogance, abundant food and careless ease, but she did not help the poor and needy" (Ezekiel 16:49, NASB). Here is the lesson of spiritual economics that all believers should take to heart. When the Lord permits the accumulation of goods beyond our need, He doesn't do it to accommodate hoarding and luxuriating, but so that those who are rich may benefit from the blessing of helping the poor. It is God's way of opening up the heart to the wonder of giving, which is central to the divine character. In this way, the believer learns by firsthand experience the truth of the proverb cited by Paul as coming from the mouth of Christ Himself: "It is more blessed to give than to receive" (Acts 20:35). Notice the apostle's instruction to the Corinthian church concerning the divine purpose in the bestowal of wealth: "You will be made rich in every way *so that* you can be generous on every occasion" (2 Corinthians 9:11; emphasis added).

Unless we are committed to being generous, wealth will be dangerous in our hands. We will be in constant peril of succumbing to the negative impact on the soul threatened by material abundance. Luxury has the tendency to corrupt spiritual life. Our hearts follow our treasure, so when we hoard for ourselves more than we can use and try to insulate our lives with things, our minds stay focused on this world and we become increasingly selfish, covetous, and defensive. Said the wise man, "Whoever loves money never has money enough," and "the abundance of a rich man permits him no sleep" (Ecclesiastes 5:10, 12). However, when we give generously to those who are in need, our hearts stay focused on God and on others.

The Mazatecs—Indians who live in southern Mexico—seldom wish each other well, and they are hesitant to teach one another. If someone were to ask the village baker who taught him to bake bread, he would reply, "I just know." The Mazatecs respond this way because the concept known as "limited good" is part of their culture. This philosophy says there is only so much good—material and otherwise—to go around, and people who share what they have with others lose it themselves. So, for instance, if people wish someone well by saying, "Have a good day!" they've given away some of their happiness forever—they'll never get it back. Similarly, the Mazatecs believe that people who teach drain themselves of knowledge; they lose it as it becomes someone else's. And in order to love a second child, parents must love their first child less.[2]

The Mazatecs aren't the only people who act this way. Their way of living is common to every culture and every heart. All of us have an instinct that prompts us to defend ourselves against want through accumulating things. It seems the more we have, the safer we feel. But that is a false perception—actually, material abundance is a narcotic that dulls the spiritual perception, putting the whole person in greater peril than if he or she drives while drunk.

Money can encourage spiritual complacency. It can breed a false sense of security and bind the heart to the things of this world. In the prophecy Jesus made concerning the final days before His return to the earth, He warned of the hindrance material possessions pose to preparedness. "On that day," He said, "no one who is on the roof of his house, with his goods inside, should go down to get them. Likewise, no one in the field should go back for anything. Remember Lot's wife!" (Luke 17:31, 32).

Scripture reveals that the way to true happiness lies in giving, not hoarding. The benefits of sharing are found in its spiritual economics, which aren't based on math. It is the concept of the material being fed by the spiritual, one realm resting upon another. The only real peace is internal, so the spirit isn't necessarily benefited by possessing an abundance of things. In fact, luxury can threaten the inner life. It was the downfall of Sodom, and though Lot and his family were worshipers of the true God, wealth became the downfall of Lot's wife and several of his children and a peril to the whole family.

In Jesus' teaching ministry, He warned repeatedly about the evil of materialism and its withering effect on the soul. For example, He dealt with it in His famous Sermon on the Mount. He warned, "No one can serve two masters. Either he will hate the one and love the other, or he will be devoted to the one and despise the other. You cannot serve both God and Money" (Matthew 6:24).

The word *Money* is capitalized in the New International Version to indicate that Jesus wasn't talking just about dollars and cents but also about the system and the power behind the money. We think we can have both God and money so long as we tithe faithfully, but Jesus makes us choose between the two. We rationalize that if we give 10 percent, the remaining 90 percent is ours to use as we please. But that is not what tithing means. God has instructed that we are to give 10 percent as a token of His ownership of the full 100 percent. God is the Owner and we are His stewards. In this way, tithe is like the Sabbath. We give God one day a week as a sign that we realize all seven days are His. Likewise, we return the tithe to show that all of "our" possessions belong to God, and He can do with them as He pleases without asking our permission. As Job said, "Naked I came from my mother's womb, and naked shall I return there. The LORD gave and the LORD has taken away; blessed be the name of the LORD" (Job 1:21, NASB).

Satan is behind the materialism that has infected our whole world. It isn't neutral; it's demonic. It encourages spiritual complacency, breeding a false sense of security. It ties our hearts to the world. Jesus purchased us with His own precious blood, but Satan draws us from His side by luring us with mansions, luxury vehicles, and stock options!

THE COST OF COMPROMISE

"When [Lot] hesitated, the men grasped his hand and the hands of his wife and of his two daughters and led them safely out of the city, for the LORD was merciful to them" (Genesis 19:16).

It is a mystery to us that Lot hesitated when his life and the lives of his family members were at stake. When he first met the strangers who came to his door, he didn't know that they weren't just men. But he certainly knew eventually—the visitors made it very clear that they'd come to destroy Sodom. And they indicated that they were on a tight timetable. Every word from their mouths communicated urgency. "Hurry, hurry," they told Lot and his family. "Flee for your lives!"

But Lot didn't hurry, and he didn't flee. Instead, he lingered. He procrastinated. He had become attached to the things he possessed, and, through close association with depraved sin, through listening to vile talk and looking at unholy things, he had lost his sense of the sinfulness of sin. Thus, he couldn't stir himself to action even to save his own life. He hadn't partaken of the sin of Sodom, but the sin of Sodom had taken a part of him.

Even though our flaws may not be as severe as Lot's or of the same kind, we must learn the overriding lesson of his experience—that being in the presence of sin so accustoms us to it that we hardly recognize it for what it is. Through sympathy with the world and its values, we come to think like those who belong to it fully and don't detect the degree to which we may have fallen away from kingdom values. Rather than leading us to criticize Lot, however worthy of criticism he may have been, his sad story should inspire us to examine ourselves.

Lot had lost his hold on spiritual reality by becoming engrossed in material things. As a result, his family, and especially his wife, became weak of spirit too. If Lot hadn't been hesitant himself, she wouldn't have looked back with longing and lost her life. And it wasn't some movement of her body, the turn of her head, that doomed her; it was what the backward look revealed about her. It showed the condition of her heart. The effect of living in luxury and of her exposure to the evil influences around her penetrated her heart more deeply than it did Lot's. So, the treasure she valued most wasn't divine deliverance. Nor was it those of her family who were saved with her. The treasure she valued most was back in Sodom, and her heart turned toward it. So weak had her spiritual nature become under the influence of wickedness that, instead of being grateful to God for sparing her life, she was angry at Him—"she rebelled against God because His judgments involved her possessions and her children in the ruin. . . . She felt that she was severely dealt with, because the wealth that it had taken years to accumulate must be left to destruction."[3]

BACKSLIDERS

When Lot's wife turned her face toward Sodom, she turned her back on Zoar, the place of refuge where the angel was leading her and her family. Her longing for the doomed city undercut her desire for the city of refuge, so that in the end she lost them both. This is an example of the dire cost of what Christians have longed called "back-sliding." Peter declares it to be worse than never having come to Christ in the first place, and the language he used to describe this perilous state reminds us of Lot's wife:

> If they have escaped the corruption of the world by knowing our Lord and Savior Jesus Christ and are again entangled in it and overcome, they are worse off at the end than they were at the beginning. It would have been better for them not to have known the way of righteousness, than to have known it and then to turn their backs on the sacred command that was passed on to them (2 Peter 2:20, 21).

Insensitivity toward something as spectacular as the divine deliverance this family experienced reveals a frightening inward condition. This story makes the jarring revelation that the regular practice of even true religion may amount to nothing more than a cultural habit that brings no spiritual benefit. It reveals the truth that carnal religion is worse than no religion at all. The heart that has been given to God and then been weaned away from Him and turned back to the world is the most to be pitied.

In the discourse that led many of Jesus' disciples to leave Him, Jesus spoke of one essential: "The Spirit gives life; the flesh counts for nothing" (John 6:63). Here He revealed the critical distinction that determines who will continue to follow Him and who will turn back. It isn't the difference between righteousness and sinfulness that distinguishes the saved from the lost; it's the difference between flesh and spirit that divides true believers from false ones. It's the difference between a disciple and a pharisee; it's the difference between Peter and Judas. There is such a thing as a "carnal" Christian—one who is born again and receives new life from God, but who, instead of overcoming the flesh, is overcome by it and follows it back into sin.[4] Peter states the problem in graphic and sobering language: "Of them the proverbs are true: 'A dog returns to its vomit,' and, 'A sow that is washed goes back to her wallowing in the mud' " (2 Peter 2:22). One commentator gives this interpretation: "The Redeemer of the world declares that there are greater sins than that for which Sodom and Gomorrah were destroyed. . . . Greater sin is theirs who profess to know God and to keep His commandments, yet deny Christ in their character and their daily life. . . . It will be more tolerable in the day of judgment for the cities of the plain than for those who have known the love of Christ, and yet have turned away to choose the pleasures of a world of sin."[5]

There is more to salvation than the distinction between good and evil. There is also the distinction between spiritual and carnal, and even those who are devout and religious and live morally impeccable lives may miss the difference. Though we attend church regularly and practice religious habits daily, our spirits may at the same time be far from God through the love of the world and adopting its values.

Jesus gave the basic lesson of redemption: "That which is born of the flesh is flesh and that which is born of the spirit is spirit." He was speaking to a highly placed, decidedly moral, and well-educated religious leader. Nicodemus was strong in the disciplines of the "church," but when Jesus explained new life to him, it became clear that he knew nothing of true spirituality. So shocking was his ignorance about salvation that Jesus commented on it, saying, "You are Israel's teacher . . . and do you not understand these things?" (John 3:10).

That night alone with Jesus opened Nicodemus's eyes to a reality he had never known before. To be sure, he was educated, but the emphasis of his religious instruction had been wrong, influenced more by tradition than by "Thus saith the Lord." This may be the weakest point of our religious training too. However sincere and devoted we may be as followers of Jesus, religious instruction of the wrong kind undermines true faith and hinders spiritual growth. Jesus referred to the story of Lot and his wife in His prophetic message about His second coming for a reason. He foresaw that in the last days all His followers would face the test of spiritual integrity that Lot's wife failed.

THE ECONOMICS OF THE LAST DAYS

The book of Revelation notes three arenas in which Satan will establish his kingdom of the last days. Revelation 13 focuses on the political arena. The whole world wonders after the beast, and the entire population of earth is required to receive a mark in either their forehead or their hand. Revelation 17 covers the religious arena, depicting it as a scarlet woman mounted on the back of the beast who makes herself drunk on the blood of the saints. Revelation 18 portrays the third arena—the economic world. The beast power is depicted as enjoying luxury—fine linen and glittering gold—and all the merchants of the earth conduct commerce with her. Then suddenly and without warning she loses her great wealth, and the world is thrown into financial chaos. "Woe! Woe, O great city, dressed in fine linen, purple and scarlet, and glittering with gold, precious stones and pearls! In one hour such great wealth has been brought to ruin!" (Revelation 18:16, 17).

This prophecy is a reminder to every believer of the temporary nature of material prosperity. None of the wealth we possess, including that bestowed directly by the hand of God, will survive the destruction of this world. The saints who are caught up to meet the Lord in the air will ascend empty-handed. All material possessions will be left behind. There'll be no baggage hold or overhead compartment in the chariot cloud that takes us to heaven, nor will there be a currency-exchange angel waiting to trade New Jerusalem coins for our dollars. The believers of the last days must learn the spiritual grace of detachment so that when they are called to do so, they can unhesitatingly let go of the material things they've had. (See Paul's confession in Philippians 4:11–13.)

LOVE AND JUDGMENT

And what of those who hang on to their sins or at least to their material goods? Does God treat them fairly?

The "burning sulfur on Sodom and Gomorrah—from the LORD out of the heavens" (Genesis 19:24) is one of the most severe punishments recorded anywhere in Scripture. It's so severe that it becomes the symbol of the ultimate destruction of the wicked in God's final eradication of sin (Jude 7). This part of the Sodom and Gomorrah drama presents serious problems for many Christians, at least for many who live in the Western world. It's a stumbling block to sincere believers who find it impossible to believe that destruction so severe as was meted out on those cities could come from the God of love.

The tendency is to think in extremes. Some define freedom as individualism. They picture God as having a love that must respect every individual without discrimination, and they believe He won't destroy or even embarrass anyone created in His image. People on the other extreme believe there's an angry, vengeful spirit full of malice, who regards no one's rights and takes pleasure in the suffering and death of humanity. What we sometimes fail to see is that the dilemma concerning the true character of God is born, not of a misunderstanding of the scriptural accounts of divine activity, but of a flawed understanding of the nature of divine love itself.

When Jesus said to Peter, "Flesh and blood did not reveal this to you" (Matthew 16:17, NASB), He was stating a principle that applies to all spiritual truth. It is divine revelation, not human intellect, that gives us the capacity to understand what happened to those cities, that it happened not by way of natural disaster but by direct divine intervention, and that what happened is consistent with the nature of God and His love. We can uphold God's love without undermining His holiness only when we understand that genuine love must set limits. Punishment, an expression of divine justice, restrains evil so that it doesn't overwhelm good.

As we read the exchanges between God and Abraham, we realize that the underlying motive in the destruction of Sodom was redemption. In response to Abraham's prodding, God keeps reducing the minimum number of redeemable souls that must be found there before He will avert judgment and save the doomed city from destruction. In the end, He says that if even ten persons can be found who aren't totally depraved by sin, He will spare the city. And when ten cannot be found and the judgment must be carried out, God sends His angels to rescue the one family that still can be saved—spiritually dull and morally compromised though they are. God never abandons His children.

Through this encounter between God and Abraham, we learn how divine love and divine holiness operate together. We can see the difference between the way God relates to His enemies and the way we relate to ours. We would destroy our enemies if we could. But God loves those He must destroy, and He hates to give them up. However, He must destroy those who have gone so far in sin as to place themselves beyond any hope of redemption. He won't allow the cancer of Sodom to continue unchecked until more and more souls are infected by it and carried beyond the reach of redemption. And God doesn't glory in the suffering of sinners or enjoy their agonies. He takes no pleasure in their death (Ezekiel 18:23).

When God judges, He is responding to the reality of sin in a fallen world. It is a fact of human nature, one that God must deal with, that human beings may reach a level of rebellion from which they can't return. Our relationship with God may reach a state that leaves Him with no alternative but to give us over to the sin we have cherished and to the consequences that sin entails (see Romans 1:18–26; 2 Thessalonians 1:9–12). Our hearts may become so hardened and our resistance to God so persistent that we cannot recover. And when we reach this place through continuing to sin deliberately, we fall irrevocably under divine condemnation.

When the sin of Sodom "reached to heaven," its cup of evil was full, and God acted to check the spread of wickedness that would corrupt the world if it were not brought to judgment. In excising the cancer of Sodom, God was being merciful. His holiness and love are not at odds with one another. His acts of judgment are acts of mercy. He destroys in order to save; He kills that He might preserve life. His holy love prompts Him to punish those He wholly loves despite their sinfulness in order to save those who may yet be saved.

It is not the repeated falling into sin because our flesh is weak that God condemns, or the feebleness of faith that causes us to break our promises again and again, despising ourselves as we do. Of this condition the Bible gives the assurance that

As a father has compassion on his children,
    so the LORD has compassion on those who fear him;
for he knows how we are formed,
    he remembers that we are dust (Psalm 103:13, 14).

But this wasn't the situation in Sodom, and we should fear the city's condition—an attitude of stubbornness in sin that provoked the righteous indignation of the Holy God. It is the determined sin of the one who has turned his back on God and resolutely walked away from Him instead of toward Him that results in a life that is irredeemably evil (Hebrews 10:26, 27). However paradoxical it may seem, God can't be true to His own character of love if He doesn't condemn sin and rebellion in those who persist in them. The experience of Moses on the mount of God may help us understand.

The nature of God

When Moses said he wanted to see God, the Almighty declared His name, and in so doing made a profound and meaningful self-revelation. In Bible times, it was often the case that one's name revealed one's nature. So, to proclaim one's name was to uncover one's innermost self. When Jacob asked God to reveal His name after the night of wrestling, God refused, saying, "Why do you ask my name?" (Genesis 32:29). But now He's ready to comply. What will He say?

He could say, "I am the Lord, the Self-Existent One." Self-existence belongs to God alone. Of all beings in the universe, only God is uncreated and uncaused, possessing unborrowed life and existing by the necessity of His own Being (John 5:26). There is no person, terrestrial or extraterrestrial, or any phenomenon of any kind that is responsible for causing God to be, nor was there ever a time when He was not. All other beings are creatures, beholden to God for their existence. God is a being, but He is not a creature: No one created Him. God alone is able to say in a completely independent and unqualified way, "I Am that I Am."

God could have announced to Moses that He is "the Lord, the Immutable One," for He is unchanging. God always is who He is. He is beyond growth and development as well as degeneration and decay. He is exalted above any kind of becoming. God alone inhabits the realm of absolute perfection, and therefore cannot improve (Psalm 102:25–27). And because change always means becoming either better or worse, God does not change.

God could have told Moses that His name is "the Lord, the Infinite One" because He is not confined to or contained within space. When we speak of divine immensity, or omnipresence, we do not mean that God is spread throughout space as though His arms were near Neptune and His feet near Mars. The laws of physics do not apply to God; we can't describe Him in terms of mass or weight or liquid or solid. God is not matter; He is spirit (John 4:24). This is a concept that we cannot visualize.

It is also true of God that He is not constrained by time; He is not in the stream of time with us. God doesn't progress along the clock from minute to minute—11:45, 11:46, 11:47—as we do, waiting to see what will happen next. He is elevated above all temporal limits and all succession of moments. He is timeless. He is not the God who was or who will be, but the God "who was, is, and is to come" (Revelation 1:8; see also Psalms 139:8; 90:2).

THE COMPASSIONATE AND GRACIOUS GOD

All of these unique perfections set God apart as the only One to be worshiped and adored with the whole heart, mind, soul, and strength. There is none like Him. Not even sinless angels can receive worship; it belongs to God alone (Revelation 19:10). But as God revealed Himself to Moses in the mountain, causing all of His glory to pass before him, God had none of these awesome perfections in mind—not divine self-existence, or immutability, or infinity.

> He passed in front of Moses, proclaiming, "The LORD, the LORD, the compassionate and gracious God, slow to anger, abounding in love and faithfulness, maintaining love to thousands, and forgiving wickedness, rebellion and sin. Yet He does not leave the guilty unpunished; He punishes the children and their children for the sin of the fathers to the third and fourth generation" (Exodus 34:6, 7).

This is the divine self-revelation. God is the One who is slow to anger yet who punishes the guilty; who abounds in love, yet who extends judgment to the third and fourth generation. It is an inescapable quandary for logic. How can anyone reconcile attributes so at odds with each other? How are we to make sense of the God of love and mercy also being the God who punishes sin through four generations? It will not do to cover one eye and pretend not to see the things that disturb us the most or to try to confine God's self-description entirely to the Old Testament, implying that somehow His character changed when Jesus came to earth. Nor can we presume that the Bible doesn't really mean what it says and that we must find a new interpretation in order to make its message relevant to our time.

Intellectualism says that rational explanations founded on sound logic can resolve all contradictions, but that is not what the Bible teaches. In Scripture, belief comes before understanding, and knowledge is founded on faith. Wisdom begins when we take God at His word and then face the truths we find with humility, however perplexing or disturbing they may seem. Acquiring wisdom doesn't mean making God fit our presuppositions; it means learning to discern God's way in the world and to adapt to it.

Wisdom is seeking to grasp spiritually the truth that is only revealed spiritually by allowing Scripture to interpret itself. And wisdom's conclusions in this case—based on the word of the Holy One Himself—are as follows: The God of mercy is also the God of justice. God revives, and God destroys. God forgives sin, and God judges sin. God brings to life, and God kills (see Deuteronomy 32:39; 1 Samuel 2:6). And in all of this He remains a God of love. Just as divine grace steps in and saves the life that has been surrendered to God, so divine judgment intervenes and cuts off the life that has rejected the Son and hardened itself against the Spirit. To say that it is like God to intervene in order to save but it isn't like God to intervene when that means judging and applying a punishment is to be inconsistent. Either God intervenes in this world or He doesn't.

It is only as God is faithful in both justice and mercy that we can see and respect His consistency so that we may obey Him out of love and not out of fear. And as we rest in God's dependability and His incorruptible holiness, our faith in Him increases, for if we couldn't trust God to keep His promise to avenge sin, how could we trust Him to keep His promise to reward the righteous? God designated two mountains as memorials of His sovereignty, Gerizim and Ebal, blessing and cursing (Deuteronomy 11:26–32). The blessing and the cursing went hand in hand. Reward and punishment were linked. We cannot have one without the other. Love that does not hate vile sin and constant rebellion is shallow and unprincipled. It cannot be trusted. It is not true love at all. Sodom was not an aberration. It demonstrated that God's immutability and infinite justice are the foundation of His love.

THE LAW OF CONSEQUENCE

The Bible speaks often and without apology about God's sovereign acts of judgment in the earth. Though sin has made its entrance, this world is still under the jurisdiction of divine law, and built into this law is the rule of consequence: In the moral world as in the physical world, every action causes a corresponding effect. It is inescapable; God's law cannot be changed. We may overlook this deed or that one, either ours or someone else's, but the law of God never overlooks sin. Every deed counts. This is why Jesus had to come to earth to reroute the penalty of sin. He bore the consequences of what we've done so that we can enjoy the consequences of what He's done for us. The law of God always applies; though the consequences may be delayed, they will show up eventually because the law of God cannot be changed or ignored. Consequently, as Scripture says, evil will have its recompense.

- "The LORD is known for justice; the wicked are ensnared by the work of their hands" (Psalm 9:16).
- "The wicked draw the sword and bend the bow to bring down the poor and needy, to slay those whose ways are upright. But their swords will pierce their own hearts, and their bows will be broken" (Psalm 37:14–15).
- "Do not be deceived: God cannot be mocked. A man reaps what he sows" (Galatians 6:7).

The law of consequence may appear to be automatic, something that happens of its own accord. That conclusion would fit with the notion of the universe as a machine—a massive apparatus running on mechanical power to manufacture the product it was designed to make. Or it may suggest karma—the sum of people's actions of the past determining a fate they can't escape. Either of these views would fit deism, the view that a divine creator brought the universe into being, provided certain laws to govern it, and then left it to run on its own.

But in other passages of Scripture, the direct divine involvement in the consequences of evil is so clearly stated as to be inescapable. As Sovereign over all the earth, God is actively engaged in its affairs. When He gave dominion over the earth to humanity, He didn't relinquish His ownership. What the Bible declares in Genesis 1:28 is not a mistake: God commanded the man and woman to "rule over the fish of the sea and the birds of the air, and over every living creature that moves along the ground." But the words of the psalmist are not mistaken either. He tells us that God has said, "Every animal of the forest is mine and the cattle on a thousand hills. . . . The world is mine and all that is in it" (Psalm 50:10, 12). The dominion humanity was given in the beginning was neither independent nor absolute. It was a position of stewardship, a secondary sovereignty under God, to whom the man and woman were always accountable. But the proximity of God to His creatures and His sovereign rule over the affairs of earth, whether in blessing or in judgment, has never been a cause of consternation for the righteous, but rather a cause of praise. The righteous rejoice in God's judgments against evil and longingly await the day when He will finally and everlastingly set things completely right (see Psalm 94, especially verses 1–7; Isaiah 42:3, 4). They understand the work of divine judgment in balancing the scales of justice so that those who are victimized by the powerful know that they have a Holy Avenger.

IN DEFENSE OF THE HELPLESS

We look upon anger and vengeance as expressions of wickedness, and so they are in the hands of sinful humanity. But God employs vengeance in defense of the helpless till righteousness is reestablished in the earth. He doesn't allow anything that harms His children to continue without consequence. He won't excuse anyone who threatens His people or causes them to suffer. His divine justice and judgment set things right again, reclaiming the universe for its Creator. "Rejoice, O nations, with his people, for he will avenge the blood of his servants; he will take vengeance on his enemies and make atonement for his land and people" (Deuteronomy 32:43). "Rejoice, saints and apostles and prophets! God has judged her for the way she treated you" (Revelation 18:20).

The truth of divine justice based on the holiness of God and the rule of divine law are attested in Scripture in ways that are impossible to ignore. A question does remain, however: How can acts that in the Bible are called vengeful be the result of love? Is not love rather acceptance, forgiveness, and healing as exemplified in the life of Jesus? When He met the woman who had been taken in adultery, He defended her against her accusers. And when the accusers were dismissed and judgment was left to Him alone, He still refrained from condemning her even though there was no question of her guilt. The woman herself never protested that she had been falsely accused, yet Jesus let her go without seeking revenge or threatening punishment.

And when Zacchaeus, a man who was universally despised as a traitor and a cheat, looked down from his perch in the tree, Jesus treated him with compassion. He didn't condemn the man's unethical financial practices, and He accepted the invitation to eat in his home even though conscientious Jews considered sitting down and eating with a publican to be an abomination. And because of Jesus' redeeming grace and love, Zacchaeus became convicted of his misdeeds and made amends for all of them, even beyond what was required.

So, we can conclude that Jesus didn't base His ministry on the threat of condemnation but on the power of divine grace. He didn't come into the world to condemn it, but that through Him it might be saved (John 3:17). This is the aspect of God's character that we have come to know. We also know that condemnation doesn't save, and often it drives away from Christ those who are trying to find their way to salvation.

As a case in point, one pastor newly appointed to a certain district decided to begin his work with a ministry of reconciliation to missing members. His first visit was to the home of a single mother who in her teens had been disfellowshiped from her church. Her daughter, born out of wedlock and now ten years old, had never attended the church of her mother's childhood. As she recounted to her new pastor the tale of her dismissal from membership at a business meeting she wasn't invited to attend and of how she was informed of the church's decision by her pastor's first-ever visit to her home, her tears began to flow. A decade after her excommunication, she was still hurting.

Then the young mother told the new minister that on the day she discovered she was pregnant, she decided to return to the church because she wanted to raise her baby in the fear of the Lord. But at the very time she was moving toward Jesus, the church pushed her aside. Had the church members reached out in love to the young mother, they would have found her to have a repentant heart and a desire to be redeemed, and no person who is willing to repent should be cut off from the body of Christ. Christians should respond to repentance with forgiveness, not rejection. This is an example of why final judgment should always be left to God, who knows the heart and reads the mind.

THE ULTIMATE EXPRESSION OF LOVE

Jesus of Nazareth is the One and only Incarnation of the true character of God; there has never been another. And Scripture says of the ultimate expression of His love in His sacrifice on the cross: "Having loved His own who were in the world, He loved them to the end" (John 13:1, NASB). But even in the life of Jesus, the most exemplary life of love the world has ever seen, the law of justice appeared. The same Jesus who preached the love of the Father and lived it out in His own life also taught that divine judgment is an aspect of God's character of love. What is probably the best-known passage of Scripture in the world states the gospel in a single sentence: "God so loved the world, that he gave his only begotten Son, that whosoever believeth in him should not perish, but have everlasting life" (John 3:16, KJV).

It's been said that if all the rest of the Bible were lost to the world, this verse would be enough to convey the gospel. Salvation is free, and it is available to all people whatever their past sins or present shame may be. But salvation isn't indiscriminate. It isn't given to all people regardless of their response to Jesus' invitation to come to Him in repentance. We must note that the element of judgment appears in the words that follow John 3:16: "Whoever believes in him is not condemned, but *whoever does not believe stands condemned already* because he has not believed in the name of God's one and only Son" (verse 18; emphasis added). "Whoever believes in the Son has eternal life, but whoever rejects the Son will not see life, for *God's wrath remains on him*" (verse 36; emphasis added).

These are the teachings of Jesus of Nazareth, whom John the Baptist introduced as "the Lamb of God who takes away the sin of the world" (John 1:29). Lambs are gentle creatures, but John said of this Lamb, "He will clear his threshing-floor, gathering his wheat into the barn and burning up the chaff with unquenchable fire" (Matthew 3:12). Shortly after Jesus' birth, "righteous and devout" Simeon held

Him in his arms and prophesied that He was to be "the child . . . destined to cause the falling and rising of many in Israel, and to be a sign that will be spoken against" (Luke 2:34). The mission of Jesus to save the world has always been steeped in mystery. It is a mystery that is penetrated not by intellect, but only by faith, and one of its central tenets is this: the coming of the Christ brings a crisis that all people must face.

The word that Jesus preaches has a double potential, an inherent two-sidedness. When Jesus was born in Bethlehem, the angels sang "peace and good will" (see Luke 2:14); but when He proclaimed His ministry publicly, He said, "I am not come to bring peace, but a sword" (Matthew 10:34). The coming of the Christ brings this paradox, a division that causes crisis. Jesus creates an emergency when He shows up. He comes in grace and love in order to save, but His coming calls people to take a stand either for Him or against Him, and by this stand we shape our eternal destiny. Notice the double potential:

- "Whosoever shall fall on this stone shall be broken; but on whomsoever it shall fall, it will grind him to powder" (Matthew 21:44, KJV).
- "Whoever believes and is baptized will be saved, but whoever does not believe will be condemned" (Mark 16:16).

Jesus is the Stone that crushes those upon whom He falls. Jesus is the Master who casts the unprofitable servant into the outer darkness, where there is weeping and gnashing of teeth (Matthew 25:30). Jesus is the King who slays those of His enemies who wouldn't accept His rule over them (Luke 19:27). And Jesus is the Lord who says to those who plead their good works before Him, "I never knew you. Away from me, you evildoers!" (Matthew 7:23).[6]

The fig tree of Mark 11 didn't die from natural causes. It didn't wither away because of the lack of rain or of nutrients. It died because Jesus cursed it as an act of judgment that prophetically symbolized His final act toward the wicked when He sits as judge of all the earth (Mark 11:14, 21). There is a holy oneness in the character of God as portrayed in the life of Jesus, a balance of both reward and punishment depending on the response of the sinners whom He came to save. God is precisely whom He reveals Himself to be, and we can't move Him into our comfort zone by remaking Him to fit our definition of love. Whether knowingly or not, those who promote divine love as grace without judgment thereby give license to sin and deny the very Lord they mean to uplift. It is bad enough to judge God, but worse still to judge Him badly.

CONTENDING FOR THE FAITH

Facing the same issue in the church of the first century, Jude contended for the authentic faith by referencing past instances of judgment that revealed the true character of God. To refute the teachings of the "certain men" who had secretly slipped in among the believers, Jude pointed back to the punishment of the unbelieving Israelites in the desert, the fate of the fallen angels now awaiting final destruction, and the destruction of Sodom and Gomorrah as an example of what those who persist in sin will suffer. It is not our place to make God fit our values. Rather, we must reorder our values to fit God as we are being transformed into the image of His Son. God's justice as revealed in judgment completes the picture of what divine love looks like in all of its paradoxical complexity. "Consider therefore the kindness and sternness of God: sternness to those who fell, but kindness to you, provided that you continue in his kindness. Otherwise, you also will be cut off" (Romans 11:22).

Once we have determined to believe in God and have begun to allow His Word to speak for itself, we find the reasons that underlie His actions, and our discovery confirms our faith in Him. It is a mistake to disassociate God's love from His holiness as though they were antithetical, as though the Judge who upholds the law thereby shows Himself to be unloving. That God is holy as well as loving is the supposed distortion of love some feel compelled to reject as giving God a bad reputation. But the logic is flawed; it doesn't uphold the integrity of Scripture. It exalts God's mercy at the expense of His justice, fragmenting the divine nature in a way that is unbiblical. Not only is it poor theology, but it is also dangerous philosophy, as we are reminded in the following quotations, which comment on the danger of romanticizing divine love:

- [By some people,] love is dwelt upon as the chief attribute of God, but it is degraded to a weak sentimentalism, making little distinction between good and evil. God's justice, His denunciations of sin, the requirements of His holy law, are all kept out of sight.[7]
- That Spirit [the Spirit of Christ] is manifested, not alone in utterances of love, compassion, and entreaty; it is not smooth things only that are spoken by holy men. God puts into the hearts and lips of His messengers truths to utter that are keen and cutting as a two-edged sword.[8]

To speak of God's mercy apart from His justice is to distort His character. We must not attempt to resolve the apparent contradiction within the divine nature by separating love from holiness. Rather, we must embrace both qualities and hold them together in tension, because while "holiness without love is severe; love without holiness is sentimental."[9] There's no tension between God's deeds of mercy and His acts of judgment; rather, God's love uses judgment to serve His righteous ends in a fallen world.

Wrath is God's strange work (Isaiah 28:21); mercy is His proper work. The one is love's only possible response to rebellion and sin; the other flows spontaneously from the heart of Him who is love, but both are works of the God of holy love who is both the Judge and the Redeemer of all humankind.[10] These twin attributes are represented in parables of Christ that seem to be in conflict.

CONFLICTING PARABLES?

In Luke 15, Jesus relates the parable of the prodigal son. In Matthew 7, He tells the story of the tree and its fruit. In the first story, the offending son is received back home with joy even though he has wasted his money and his life in riotous living. In the second story, religious people, churchgoers, are banished from God's presence even though they have performed miraculous deeds in Jesus' name. The two narratives present depictions of divinity that seem to be at odds with each other until we realize that, when they are taken together, they show the completeness of God's character.

Parables are metaphors meant to convey one main point of truth.

The parable of the rich man and Lazarus is proof enough that even in Christ's parables, not every detail is meant to depict reality (Luke 16:19–31). Both the parable of the prodigal son and the parable of the tree and its fruit reveal the character of God, but each parable pictures only one aspect of His character. The God who welcomes home the wayward boy is the same God who banishes the self-sufficient disciples, and He is neither indulgent in the one case nor arbitrary in the other. We see the complete picture of God's character only as the various pieces of the puzzle are fitted together in just the right way.

God is both loving and exacting, both merciful and just, both forgiving and condemning. How He treats us depends on our attitudes and responses. He is the only Person who exhibits these apparently contradictory character traits in the exact balance that constitutes holy love. This is the God of Scripture, and any attempt to alter His character, to "dumb it down" to our level of understanding, even though propelled by an honest motive, ends up playing into the hands of the tempter. Ellen White warned,

> Satan deceives many with the plausible theory that God's love for His people is so great that He will excuse sin in them; he represents that while the threatenings of God's word are to serve a certain purpose in His moral government, they are never to be literally fulfilled.[11]

She sharply refuted such a misrepresentation of the balance of love and wrath we find in God's character:

> The unconditional pardon of sin never has been, and never will be. Such pardon would show the abandonment of the principles of righteousness, which are the very foundation of the government of God. . . . God has faithfully pointed out the results of sin, and if these warnings were not true, how could we be sure that His promises would be fulfilled? That so-called benevolence which would set aside justice is not benevolence but weakness.[12]

God's nature is love; that's who He is in His Being (1 John 4:16).

Wrath is God's tool, but it isn't His nature. It doesn't describe God as He is in Himself; it only describes God as He relates to sinners who spurn His love and do despite to His grace. Rejecting them brings pain to His heart (Genesis 6:6).

Wrath is God's holy resolve to destroy sin and all who cling to it. It is His fierce and decisive opposition to evil. It is true that where there is no love there is no God, but it is also true that where there is no wrath there is no love.[13] Love must hate evil or it is complicit with it. Thus Scripture depicts God as One who hates haughty eyes, a lying tongue, hands that shed innocent blood, the heart that devises wicked schemes, and so on (see Proverbs 6:17, 18). "God is a just judge, and God is angry with the wicked every day" (Psalm 7:11, NKJV).

Divine love is eternal, and "God is love" is the most fundamental and profound affirmation that can be made about God. Divine wrath, on the other hand, is only temporary. When God has finally put an end to sin, His anger against sin will no longer be needed. God had no holy vengeance before the world fell into sin, and when the universe is made whole again, divine wrath will cease to exist.

God's hatred of evil stands beside His love of righteousness. Divine holiness demands justice, and God cannot deny Himself. But the vengeance of God is not like our vengeance, which is why the Bible tells us to let God repay those who hurt us in one way or another (Romans 12:19; Hebrews 10:30, 31). He knows how to avenge justly, and we don't. The hatred we express as sinners is malevolent, filled with rancor and ill will. It retaliates against its enemies, wishes for the worst to happen to them, and then takes pleasure in their suffering. No such feelings and actions accompany God's wrath. Scripture makes clear that in our fallen condition, even at our best, we can never fully comprehend the divine character. It is a mystery to us. Like Lot, our spiritual sensibilities have been numbed by the effect of sin both from without and from within. "[Lot] did not realize the terrible necessity for God's judgments to put a check on sin,"[14] and neither do we. In fact, judgment is God's love in its operation against sin.

THE OPPOSITE OF LOVE

The opposite of love is not hatred. The opposite of love is apathy—the complete lack of interest in or concern for the other. God is opposed to everything that hurts or destroys His people, and He can no more stand by now and watch sin go unpunished than He could have stood by in the beginning and watched the world become the eternal domain of Satan. So often we refrain from speaking hurtful truths to others because of what it would cost us. We justify our silence on crucial issues by telling ourselves that we have no right to judge someone else, when in reality the greater motivation is our unwillingness to place ourselves in a position that involves conflict. To love is not to stay uninvolved out of respect for someone's rights or personal freedom. To love is to intervene in defense of the powerless and disadvantaged and for the salvation of the one who is committing the evil.

In his letter to the Corinthians, Paul explained that confrontational love is an act of salvation, not destruction. Silence in the face of wrongdoing is destructive both to the individual and to the community. It is the unwillingness to hurt that does the most harm. Paul rebuked the Corinthians for their failure to correct a brother among them who was engaging in open sin, "a kind that does not occur even among pagans: A man has his father's wife" (1 Corinthians 5:1). By failing to act on this matter, the church was abdicating its responsibility to love one of their brothers with the love of Christ.

When we shy away from a worthy fight, not out of conviction that the fight is wrong but because we want to avoid trouble, we have acted against the principle of love. We have shown that our comfort is more important to us than the discomfort of speaking up to an erring brother or sister in the hope that they might be saved through loving confrontation. On the other hand, when we put ourselves out there for the sake of someone else, risking the loss of that person's friendship, we have shown a love that breaches the comfort zone for the good of someone else. We have acted as Jesus acted.

In addition to the theological arguments for understanding God's judgments as love, there are also sociological considerations to take into account. It's easy for us who live among the privileged in the richest country in the world to invent a God who is too sensitive to risk offending us and too respectful to infringe on our personal rights; a God who regards us as equals and leaves us to take charge of our own affairs. But even in this we show our hypocrisy, for when it is our family at risk, we want a different God. When our child is the victim of abuse and the perpetrator gets off on some technicality, we don't want a sensitive God. When our nation goes to war and our freedoms are at stake along with the preservation of our way of life, then we pray for a God who will fight on our side and help us destroy the enemy. We realize then that we, on our own, can't manage the world or even our lives effectively, that we need the Sovereign God who performs justice in the earth based on His character of unbiased love. If God doesn't rise up and judge sinners; if He doesn't come to the rescue of the helpless who cry to Him day and night—the exploited children, the dehumanized women, the victims of violence, oppression, and genocide—if the Holy God doesn't take up His sword and finally destroy sin and sinners, then He would be guilty of indifference and could not be the God of love.

We must be careful that our position as the predominant culture in the world doesn't lead us to idolize our culture. We must be careful so that our position in the world as the one remaining superpower doesn't beguile us into thinking we have the ascendancy in the kingdom of God as well. We must be careful not to fall into the subtle deception of interpreting the Bible by our standards as a "Christian nation"; we must instead allow Scripture to interpret Scripture. We must be humble enough that when we cannot explain God's Word, we accept what we cannot understand by faith, which is the substance of things hoped for, the evidence of things not seen (Hebrews 11:1). While we claim to be believers who possess new light, we must be careful not to allow arrogance to turn us into unbelievers. The old dictum still rings with truth, "Let God be God and all men be liars."

A TRAGIC, HUMAN STORY

Sodom is a tragic human story. Through the weaknesses and failures of the family of Lot we learn that luxury, compromise, and carnal religion expose us to the same peril as those who are outright enemies of God must face. But in the midst of all the fire and brimstone there is something different on the divine side—an encouraging ray of hope, one more thing for us to see. "When he hesitated, the men grasped his hand and the hands of his wife and of his two daughters and led them safely out of the city, for the LORD was merciful to them. As soon as they had brought them out, one of them said, 'Flee for your lives! Don't look back, and don't stop anywhere in the plain! Flee to the mountains or you will be swept away!' " (Genesis 19:16, 17). Verse 16 speaks of "the men," plural; in verse 17, it is "one of them." After Lot and his family were in the clear, the two angels who had visited them turned back to perform their work of destruction. It was Jesus who gave the final warning. After He had finished His prolonged discussion with Abraham, He came to make sure Lot and his family were safe.

In the midst of destruction, the hand of Jesus brought redemption, and once again we marvel at His amazing grace. Lot was no faith giant like his uncle Abraham. He wasn't called the friend of God; nor was he promised descendants like the sand of the sea. He was an ordinary believer riddled with weaknesses like you and me, but the Lord didn't leave him to destruction. God was patient with Lot's feebleness, his wavering faith, and his outright lack of gratefulness. He remembered that Lot was only dust. The Lord is patient with us too. He bears long with our foolish ways as we repeat the same mistakes again and again. He commits Himself to saving us in spite of our halting slowness to respond to Him, and we glory in His unfailing love.

But what of our commitment to Him? Are we as faithful with our devotion to Christ as He is in His devotion to us? Do we renew our commitment to Him every day and keep ourselves ever before Him, immersing our whole lives in His love and bringing every thought into captivity to obedience to Him? (2 Corinthians 10:5). Are we careful not to take our salvation for granted just because we go to church—realizing that following religion may not be the same as following Jesus? God reveals His love both in blessing and cursing, in redeeming and destroying, in taking to heaven and in condemning to hell, but we don't need to fear the negative response that is temporary until sin is eradicated. We may live in the light of positive attributes that are as eternal as God Himself is eternal. Then we will be at peace with God and feel no need to change His holy nature in order not to be afraid.

If there were a contest for the most unique country in the world, the winner might be Greenland. It is the largest island in the world. Eighty percent of its land mass is covered with ice, which in some places is ten thousand feet thick. It is the least populated country in the world, and though it's closer to North America, it is a dependent territory of Denmark. Apparently, it got its name, a misnomer, from early settlers who wanted to attract other people. (Icelanders, on the other hand, named their country to keep outsiders away!)

The freezing waters around Greenland contain countless icebergs. Their movements are paradoxical. While the small ice floes move in one direction, the massive icebergs move in another—they move in different directions though they're on the same sea!

There's an explanation. The small icebergs are driven by surface winds and currents, but deep ocean currents move the massive icebergs. Two forces in the same sea are pushing in different directions.

In the spiritual realm, too, our lives are subject to two forces. The love of God is as consistent as God's nature is unchanging, but love's effect on repentance differs from its impact on rebellion and stubbornness. If God's love reacted in the same way toward the unrepentant as toward the repentant, then God would be inconsistent. We can count on God's love to be eternally the same and to always be receptive to the ones who are willing to admit their wrongs and repent. That same love, faithful to the end, will see us safely into the eternal kingdom, where neither sin nor wrath will exist anymore forever.

SACRIFICE: ABRAHAM AND ISAAC
CHAPTER 8

Abraham called that place The LORD Will Provide.
—Genesis 22:14

Paradoxes interest me because the fact that they exist says logic doesn't have all the answers. Logic abhors contradictions, and the fact that it does so shows that it has limitations. It says that proposition X and proposition Not X cannot both be true, yet a paradox is defined as a valid deduction from an acceptable premise that leads to a contradiction—for instance, that X and Not X are both true. Even describing the theory agitates our logical minds!

The liar's paradox illustrates the problem more clearly. In one version of this paradox, the conundrum is a line that reads, "This sentence is false." Is that line true or false? If it's false, then it's true, and if it's true, then it's false!

Here's another example of a liar's paradox. Picture an index card containing two simple sentences, one on each side of the card. The sentence on one side reads, "The statement on the other side of this card is true," and the sentence on the other side reads, "The statement on the other side of this card is false." You can flip that card over and back all day long and never resolve the paradox!

The point is that logic, reason, can't explain everything. There are truths in the spiritual realm that reason alone cannot understand, either deductively or inductively—consequently, another kind of reasoning is called for: namely, the reasoning of faith. And the best example of the reasoning of faith comes in the story of the test that God applied to Abraham—"the closest which man was ever called to en-dure."[1] "God said, 'Take your son, your only son, Isaac, whom you love, and go to the region of Moriah. Sacrifice him there as a burnt offering on one of the mountains I will tell you about' " (Genesis 22:2).

THE COMMAND

Abraham sits straight up in his bed, startled out of sleep. Beads of perspiration dampen his brow as a chill of horror makes him shudder. The divine command is totally unexpected; it comes out of nowhere and staggers the old man like an unseen left hook. And the language God uses seems calculated to stir up Abraham's deepest fatherly emo-tions: "Take now your son, your only son, whom you love . . ."

God knows exactly how much He's asking, but Abraham can't see it. He has sacrificed lambs on the altar countless times. He knows the procedure. He tries to imagine it now: his hand rising as he prepares to strike the lethal blow, his fingers trembling as he tightens his grip, his heart pounding as he begins the downward stroke, the weapon whistling as he accelerates it with lethal intent. He tries to see it all the way through to the end—the blade piercing the precious flesh, the blood spurting out in every direction, his beloved son grunting and then gasping for his last breath—but his thoughts break off. His mind will not continue. And he wonders, *If I can't even think about it, how in the world will I ever be able to bring myself to do it?*

As the old man rises and begins to pack, he reflects on the events that have filled the half century of his life since he took up with this invisible God. On the strength of a promise, he left all that was famil-iar to journey to an unknown land. When he got there, God said that one day it would all be his someday, but for fifty years he has lived in a tent without having an acre to call his own.

But Abraham has believed God, and the Lord has prospered him and made his name great. Even the rulers in Beersheba respect him as a prince and a man of integrity. The sheep and cattle he owns cover the plains. Hundreds of servants wait to fulfill his every wish. And best of all, for the past twenty years his family life has finally been made complete with Sarah, the wife of his youth, and Isaac, the son of his old age. Abraham is now in repose, having received at last the gift for which he waited so long. His brother Nahor might have twelve sons, but Abraham and Sarah are happy to have one of their own. Everything has been going so well that Abraham has been thinking his final years might well be the most peaceful of all.

But now this.

THE RESPONSE OF FAITH

The response of the aged patriarch amazes us. He doesn't complain, and he doesn't hesitate. He doesn't consult Sarah. He doesn't confide in his favorite servant. He doesn't even tell Isaac what's really going on. He simply sets out to do what God has commanded.

One more thing: Abraham doesn't even consult with himself. He doesn't linger to wallow in self-pity. There is no equivocating, no rationalizing, and no sentimentalism; there is only faith in action. This beginning—an old patriarch starting out on a painful journey he doesn't understand without a single person in whom to confide—is testament to an enormous faith.

Aside from being painful even in its anticipation, the command of God presents troubling tasks for the old man: *Familial*—what will he say to his wife, and how will she react? *Social*—how will he explain his actions to his friends? But also *spiritual*—Abraham hasn't known the true God to require or even to accept human sacrifice. Never mind what others will think; the bigger question is how he'll explain this to himself. Can this command really be from God? Every instinct and sensibility that Abraham has, along with every rational thought, prejudices him against this directive. Yet he knows it is God's command. So, exhibiting a faith that seems superhuman, he sets out to obey it. Abraham's faith in what he heard and from whom he heard it is more important to him than any other consideration. Even when he cannot understand God's purpose, he goes on.

When we can't easily distinguish between right and wrong, we enter what is sometimes called a "gray area" of life—a place where light and darkness mix. We know gray areas actually are a matter of our perception, because light and darkness always differ radically. Scripture emphasizes this point: "God is light; in him there is no darkness at all" (1 John 1:5) So, when we can't see clearly the place where the darkness ends and the light takes over, we must rely on faith— "the evidence of things not seen" (Hebrews 11:1, KJV). We follow the example of Abraham and walk in the way of God's command, believing that as we exercise the obedience of faith, we will eventually see the light at the end of the tunnel, and the way will be made clear once more. The gray area is a faith test, an opportunity to exercise obedience, strengthen our relationship with God, and sharpen our spiritual perception.

My wife was teaching our nephew the different positions on the dial of the room fan—High, Low, and Off—and little David was fascinated. At first he called out the words after her, repeating what she said as she turned the dial from one position to the next: "High!" "Low!" "Off!" Before long he was doing it by himself, turning the dial and correctly identifying the positions even though he was too young to read. But as he mastered the task, his curiosity took hold and cried out for more. So he pushed the envelope. He turned the dial to a position between High and Low, a position for which there was no label, and then he looked at my wife with a quizzical brow as if to ask, "What do you call this one?" Januwoina hesitated. She didn't know how to explain this limbo to a two-year-old. It wasn't High, and it wasn't Low. Finally, believing that he wasn't quite ready yet to grasp such a concept, she pushed the dial through its stops and repeated as before "High," "Low," "Off," and David seemed satisfied to be back on familiar ground.

Life is full of these gray areas, and just as was true of our little nephew, the immature are not ready to handle them, to navigate them properly as followers of God. When we aren't ready for the complexity of gray, we tend to revert to familiar ground, to something that makes us comfortable, the unambiguous patches of black and white, even though the situation we're in may be anything but unambiguous. Unable to navigate the bleakness of the gray, we begin to look for mechanical matters, settling for the superficiality of regulations, never probing beneath the surface to grapple with the complex issues for which simple rules are inadequate. We treat reality as though it were black and white—insisting on it in fact—even while we criticize as "unprincipled" those who move more cautiously as they try to navigate a clear path through murky waters.

For Abraham, there was no room for self-deception; there was only obedience or disobedience, and obedience cost more than it had at any other time in his life. To carry out the command of God this time would cost everything that was dearest to him—his fatherhood, the son who was heir to the promise, and probably his wife's love and confidence as well. All obedience involves sacrifice, even if we're sacrificing only the good opinion of a friend who doesn't understand what we're doing or why. But obedience costs the most when it requires us to sacrifice what we love most.

"On the third day Abraham looked up and saw the place in the distance" (Genesis 22:4).

The sight of those mountains pierced Abraham like the thrust of a dagger. He'd have to go through with it after all. He hadn't slept since God's command had come to him. He had passed each night in prayer, pleading for clarification, for further explanation, but none came. It seemed the sky had turned to stone, and his prayers weren't getting through.

ON UNCHARTED WATERS

Seeing Abraham's experience, we come to understand something of the nature of pioneering faith. Abraham was sailing uncharted waters—there were no inspired writings to which he could look for guidance, no salvation history to show him what to do. He was making the history as he went, following faith without sight. But perplexed as he was, he still followed on. Abraham shuddered. Abraham trembled. But Abraham obeyed God. He didn't understand what was going on, but he knew the One who had commanded him, and that was enough. He didn't have the comfort of knowing that this was the final test, one that would bring his faith to full maturity. He knew only the conflict that was raging now. It wasn't a conflict between good and evil. It wasn't a test about distinguishing right from wrong. The struggle within Abraham was between natural life and spiritual life—a struggle that is common to all believers; one that is the central issue of the experience of sanctification.

The great test of obedience for the mature believer lies not in separating darkness from light, but in pushing through the gray until the light appears at the end of the tunnel, or in this case, at the summit of the mountain. It's one thing to deny our sinful self. It is another thing to deny self when we know that we haven't sinned but have acted in accordance with God's commands. David could accept the death of his son as a punishment for his sin in taking Bathsheba as his wife and sending her husband to his death. But even in that circumstance he didn't acquiesce to the consequences easily—he fasted and prayed for his son to be spared. But when the infant died, David got up, washed himself, ate, and submitted to God's will (2 Samuel 12:15–23). Abraham, on the other hand, knew that since he had been one hundred years old when his son was conceived, only the power of God's Spirit had given him that son. Isaac was the long-awaited fulfillment of God's promise, the heir of the covenant through whom the Promised One would come. That Isaac would be taken from him was the last thing Abraham expected. God's intent was that through experiencing the severest test of faith imaginable, a test that Abraham couldn't pass by following reason alone, he would reach the heights of sanctification. This is precisely where many of us part company with Abraham.

A theology professor who holds a PhD in philosophy begins one of his classes with a revealing illustration. He raises a jar full of beans and asks his students to guess how many beans are in the jar and then write their name and their estimate on a piece of paper—and next to it, write the name of their favorite song. When all the students have written down their guesses, the professor reveals the number of beans in the jar, and, of course, the students look to see whose estimate was closest to being right. Then the professor asks another question—he asks who was right about the favorite song. Generally, the students say, correctly, that's not a matter of right or wrong; it's a matter of taste. At this point the professor asks a question that's really the point of the whole exercise—he asks whether their decisions regarding what to believe about God and their faith are more like estimating the number of beans in the jar or more like choosing their favorite song. Invariably, he gets the same answer from young and old. They say that deciding questions of faith is more like choosing their favorite song; it's a matter of taste and of personal preference.

A recent survey by the Barna Research Group confirms the conclusion of this anecdote. To the question "Is there absolute truth?" 66 percent of Americans (72 percent of those ages 18–25) say No. They say that people can define truth in contradictory ways and still all be correct. As we're considering Abraham's experience with God, let's do so with these questions in mind: Is faith in God a simple matter of choice, one that varies from person to person? And is it relative or absolute—and if it is relative, does that make God relative too?

Obedience is an essential part of the life of faith, and sometimes that means obeying without understanding completely the reason behind God's command. But when His command moves from arbitrary to contradictory—not just without an apparent reason but against reason itself—and even appears to flout morality, we cannot obey. Our sense of personal rights won't permit us to obey a command we can neither understand nor respect. These are the kinds of issues that not only disturb us, but also make it difficult for us to share our faith with coworkers and friends—intelligent people who insist that an idea be logical before they will accept it.

Of differing domains

We might attempt to solve the problem by saying that faith and reason have different areas of authority, each limited to enabling us to discern the truth only within its domain. This is the suggestion that then Senator Barack Obama made in the book in which he used the Abraham and Isaac story as an example. He modernized the story and placed it in a Western context. He wrote,

> If any of us saw a 21st century Abraham raising the knife on the roof of his apartment building, we would call the police; we would wrestle him down; even if we saw him lower the knife at the last minute, we would expect the Department of Children and Family Services to take Isaac away and charge Abraham with child abuse.[2]

Senator Obama used this illustration to argue that politics calls for a modification of faith into something all people can understand, even those who do not share the same faith. He admits, however, that his conclusion isn't based on universal law but on the particular political realities of our culture. "In a pluralistic democracy," he says, "we have no choice." His conclusion, then, is one of pragmatism not of faith.

However, believers must take more than practicality into consideration, and they must do so without disregarding the laws and the norms of the society in which they live—a difficult assignment. Scripture commands believers to respect and obey civil authorities as those who have been appointed by God, while other Scripture passages tell us that when civil authority and a divine mandate take divergent paths, God expects His disciples to obey God rather than humans (Romans 13:1; compare Acts 4:18–20; 5:29).

Sooner or later every believer must come to terms with the innate tension between the wisdom of God and the wisdom of the world. Scripture clearly warns about it. The temptations that difference brings appear in every generation and appeal to every culture, including ours, the post-Enlightenment West. The received wisdom of our day conflicts with the wisdom of God, and to accept this truth and embrace it is one of the unrecognized hurdles of the self-abandonment salvation requires. It is so difficult for us because it implies that our intellects are inadequate. Don't underestimate the challenge this truth poses to our self-image; we have a desperate need to hold on to the pride of our opinions. We think of ourselves as intelligent persons and as beings made in God's image—which is just what we should believe. But we find that our intelligence is inadequate to attaining spiritual truths. The Bible says that only fools understand. Saving faith has a recklessness about it that refuses to be restrained; a recklessness that is willing to take a leap without a guarantee of a safe or profitable landing. Intellectualism wants to be in control, and in its pride won't accept anything it can't explain. It insists on the rule of rationality. But intellectualism can't save us. Faith by its very nature operates in the vacuum of reason's unanswered questions, which are manifold. Faith itself is the missing evidence.

"Where is the wise? Where is the scribe? Where is the disputer of this age? Has not God made foolish the wisdom of this world?" "The foolishness of God is wiser than men, and the weakness of God is stronger than men" (1 Corinthians 1:20, 25, NKJV).

The Bible is not merely a religious book we read for our devotions—it is a window on reality. It is the "Book of books" because it stands within the unique genre of "spiritual truth." The Bible alone tells us the truth about our world and ourselves. What we see and hear is not ultimately real. We can't access reality through the senses. We know only the world of our perceptions, and our perceptions are limited because of our finitude and distorted because of our sin. But in the Word of God the veil is lifted, and by the illumination of the Holy Spirit, we see things as they really are, and we're empowered to live on the only basis endorsed in the Word: "The just shall live by faith" (Habakkuk 2:4; Romans 1:17, KJV).

Those who take the path of intellectualism assume that knowledge can be measured by tests. That path is the province of well-trained minds, whose academic achievements are celebrated. In the pathway of revelation, knowledge is not a matter of the intellect at all, but of a relationship with God. It is not the light that shines from within that illuminates the path of truth; it is the light that shines in from outside of ourselves. It is the heart that has been surrendered to God and trained to be always open to Him that can receive the light of truth. How wise believers become is determined by the closeness of their walk with Christ.

All those who want to live as people of faith must face challenges. When the rational decide that the only reality is material reality, they create a conflict. When science asserts that nature is all there is, it establishes a limitation faith cannot accept. When God sends His Word to us, He requires us to believe it primarily because it is His Word. This is the only rationality He will approve—the common sense that accepts the word of the Creator over everything else creation may appear to be saying.

Change of rank

There was a time when, in Western culture, religion was studied right alongside mathematics and science with no thought of any contradiction between them. But the worldview of our culture has changed; theology is no longer ranked with the sciences and is in fact no longer taken seriously. Now the Western world looks to the ancient Greek philosophers as the fount of wisdom and takes for granted the superiority of the rational process.

When the scientific community comes to consensus on anything, its conclusions are treated as irrefutable fact. All branches of learning, including theology, adapt to their findings. So those who want to be respected for their intelligence have to stand in the Greek stream of thought. Yet the first letter addressed to the Corinthians asserts that the message of salvation is not dependent on the thinking of the intelligentsia of the time: "Jews request a sign, and Greeks seek after wisdom; but we preach Christ crucified, to the Jews a stumbling block and to the Greeks foolishness" (1 Corinthians 1:22, 23).

The city of Corinth was a commercial powerhouse of the first-century world, a dynamic center of trade. It stood on an overland route used by merchants who wanted to avoid the dangerous voyage around the Peloponnesus, which was subject to violent storms. They would unload their cargo at a port on the Saronic Gulf, cross the narrow isthmus to the Gulf of Corinth, and reload their cargo onto ships to continue the journey west. All the traffic made Corinth a bustling, cosmopolitan city, and the Christian church at Corinth reflected the diversity of the city.

Athens was just over fifty miles away, and that sophisticated city had a strong influence on Corinth. As one historian put it, the scent of Stoicism was in the air; it was part of the common coinage of life and its everyday exchanges. The basic form of education was rhetoric—the art of persuasion based on logic and reason. This form of intelligence was highly prized.

The Greeks believed in the elevation of the human race; they thought it could be accomplished only through the study of science and philosophy. This was the bias Paul sought to redress by his persistence in presenting the gospel on another ground. "I determined to know nothing among you except Jesus Christ, and Him crucified," he said (1 Corinthians 2:2, NASB). Paul used neither the substance nor the form of the philosophic categories of his day to present the message of salvation. Like the other apostles of Jesus, he refused to adopt the commonly accepted wisdom of the day. Instead, they wrote within a perspective provided by the Spirit of God, not quoting the "wisdom" of any of the philosophers, but presenting spiritual truths in spiritual words.

Paul's frame of reference was not intellectualism; it was the demonstration of the Spirit's power in witnessing to the Son of God—because "spiritual things are spiritually discerned." This is why the Bible doesn't fit our modern categories of thought and why we can't make it fit—not because it is ancient and outmoded, but because it is of a different nature.

The wisdom of God is not a product of the intellect. In theology, objective truth is what God knows. He's the Omniscient One by whom all human knowledge is to be evaluated and judged. This explains why there is no epistemology in the New Testament—no investigating of the knowledge base to determine which beliefs are justified and which are not. Every thought of God is reality, and the truths of God taught in His Word are eternal, immutable, and unimpeachable, and we must relate to them as such.

God isn't concerned with satisfying our intellectual curiosity. He's more concerned about telling us what we need to know to get out of this world alive. The divine agenda is the salvation of as many as possible—of "whosoever will." And here we find the miracle of divine revelation: God has made it possible for all of us to receive His wisdom by direct communion with Him. It is Spirit-to-spirit contact—God's Spirit touching our spirit directly and thus illuminating our minds and hearts with divine light. Paul says the thoughts of God become our thoughts. In fact, Paul makes the astounding claim that "we have [Greek: *echomen*] the mind of Christ" (1 Corinthians 2:16). In the Greek, the base word, *echō*, is a strong term that means "I seize," "I possess," "I cling to." This word denotes internal possession. As God's Spirit—the great Revealer of God—possesses us, we possess God's mind. This is a different concept than our culture teaches us. It's something new: knowledge we obtain not by intellect but by relationship; not by what we know but by who knows us.

Hidden from the Wise

Once, when Jesus was explaining to His disciples the reason He used parables to teach, He said, "I praise you, Father, Lord of heaven and earth, because you have hidden these things from the wise and learned and revealed them to little children. Yes, Father, for this was your good pleasure" (Matthew 11:25, 26). When we're seeking human knowledge, we look to the Greeks and their offspring—the scientists, the philosophers, and the experts in rhetoric. But when we want to know God, we must imitate children. Their simple understanding is based on personal contact. Their ready faith makes them quick to believe whatever they're told by someone they trust. They follow even when they don't know where they are being led. And when they suffer doubt or fear, they cling all the more tightly to the one leading them.

The knowledge of God is relational and not intellectual; consequently, because we know things intuitively, we can understand things we can't explain. God gives these things to us as matters of personal trust. He makes known to us the utterly unsearchable mysteries of divinity. We don't uncover these mysteries through the working of our intellects so we can take pride in our discovery, turn it into a formula, publish it, win a book award, and then mass-produce the book, sell it on the open market, and make a fortune. It isn't that kind of wisdom, nor is it for that purpose. It is the wisdom of God made ours through a miraculous relationship initiated on the divine side by an act of grace, received on the human side through the obedience of faith, and lived out in the everyday life through the harmony of "two become one" in the unique existence known as the Christian life. It is the life that is mediated through death—the death of the self.

Abraham was aware of these things as he made his torturous journey. Known as the "friend of God," he was known as well as the "father of the faithful," and these two names are interrelated. It was because of Abraham's dependency upon God—his trust and complete obedience—that he possessed the faith to endure the trial he faced on top of Mount Moriah. It was the intuitive knowledge he had acquired through years of walking with God that sustained him as he made his way there. Abraham remembered that everything that happens to the believer is in the context of covenant, and covenant begins with the God who can be trusted implicitly. This is its first principle. God is sovereign in the plan of salvation just as He is in creation. And our salvation is found in this: that once and for all we should learn to put God at the center of everything in our lives and say with conviction, "Whatever God does He does well; all of His works are righteousness!" Here is the truth that Abraham was living, grinding it out on his knees through sleepless nights. And still he must go through the dreadful ordeal of seeing it to the end.

"Abraham took the wood for the burnt offering and placed it on his son Isaac, and he himself carried the fire and the knife" (Genesis 22:6). Together Abraham and Isaac ascend to the summit; the younger man carrying the heavier load, the older man the more dangerous load, and every step bringing them closer to God. The symbolism of the Cross is unmistakable: the son bears the wood on his back, the father carries the fire in his hands. Together they build the altar and arrange the wood, with no lamb in sight. And now comes the moment of truth. Abraham must reveal what is really going on—and Isaac is no child. He is a young, vibrant man. He can escape this fate if he chooses to. No one can force him. But Isaac is a sharer in his father's faith, and he submits without complaining. He actually considers it an honor to be sacrificed as an offering for God's glory.[3]

Abraham must now enact what he has dreaded for three days. He stretches his son out on the wood, and then he closes his eyes and reviews what he knows. He knows that God is good, and he knows that God always keeps His word. That means that somehow, Isaac will live. Perhaps God will resurrect him; maybe that is His plan (Hebrews 11:19). So, Abraham determines that whatever pain he must suffer, he will hold nothing back from God—not even his son.

So, Abraham and Isaac bid each other farewell in a trembling embrace. Then the young man prostrates himself, and the old man straightens up. The son exposes his throat, and the father stretches out his hand—and we close our eyes, unable to watch. And at the height of Abraham's reach, just as he is about to strike, a voice sounds from heaven: "Abraham! Abraham! Do not lay a hand on the child. Now I know that you fear God, for you have not withheld your son from Me" (see Genesis 22:11, 12). So Paul's pronouncement: "Abraham believed God, and it was credited to him as righteousness" (Romans 4:3). And the meaning of the gospel comes home to us. God didn't desire Isaac's death; He wanted Abraham's life. God provided Himself a Lamb. The agony of separation between Father and Son was not Abraham's and Isaac's; it was God's. And Abraham was transformed by the experience, but not by his own merit. He was changed because he put his trust in God, the One who saves by His own blood.

A contract is based on merit and depends on performance. But the divine covenant that provides salvation to us is not a contract in which two parties engage in reciprocal activity that is mutually beneficial; a contract in which both sides have obligations and both sides benefit. The scholars who produced the Septuagint—the translation of the Old Testament from Hebrew into Greek—could choose among several Greek words to translate the Hebrew term *berit*. The standard Greek word was *synthēkē*. But that word with its connotation of agreement between equals was unsuitable. It didn't fit the plan of salvation. So the translators settled on another word: *diathēkē*, "will" or "testament"—a word that describes a disposition of goods by one person upon another. In this word we see the dominant idea of the divine covenant—one-sidedness. In the plan of salvation, everything depends on God. He provides Himself a lamb—the Lamb of God is Jesus. And that isn't all; the word *diathēkē* also describes a decision that is irrevocable; one that no one can cancel. Glory to God! Our salvation rests on a sovereign act of the Sovereign God, and no power can take us out of His hand.

Everything is staked on God, not on us. The great God of heaven and earth—who has no need of heaven or earth—swears upon Himself to redeem us and abide with us forever. The King puts on the beggar's clothes and goes out to convince the beggar that He is on his side. This is the incomprehensible love of God, love that is all the greater because we have no claim on it. God doesn't owe it to us, and we don't deserve it. It comes by grace.

"THE LORD WILL PROVIDE"

"Abraham called the name of that place The LORD Will Provide. And to this day it is said, 'On the mountain of the LORD it will be provided' " (Genesis 22:14).

"The mountain of the LORD"—that line is significant. The mountain is Moriah, and we are to hear that name again. On that sacred spot Solomon will break ground for the building of the temple where sacrifices will be offered for a thousand years. And on that same spot a lamb about to be offered up for the forgiveness of the sins of God's people will run free when Jesus of Nazareth makes the ultimate sacrifice on a cross outside the walls of the city. But that sacrifice won't be like this one. No one will shout "Enough!" when the crucified Jesus suffers. No one will rescue Him at the last moment, saying that it was only a test. Jesus will have to go through with it all the way to the end. Jesus will pay it all.

Two brothers walking home from school were surrounded by a gang of bullies. The bullies didn't beat them; instead, they tied them up and left them in an abandoned field. The brothers felt lucky to have escaped a beating until they realized they couldn't free themselves. Time passed, the sun set, night fell, and the boys were still in their bonds. Then they heard footsteps coming toward them in the dark, and they heard their names being called by a familiar voice—the voice of their father. When they didn't come home after school, he had begun to search for them. He searched through the last of the daylight hours and into the night, but he found his boys and brought them home.

We often think of Jesus and the great sacrifice He made for us and for the world. We realize that we don't understand it at all—what it must have been like to take on the sin of the whole world. The very idea makes us shudder. But because of the physical suffering He endured, we can at least identify with Jesus and count ourselves to have participated in His sufferings when we ourselves have to go through pain and loss for the glory of His name. But with God the Father, the story is different. We don't often think of the Father's suffering when He had to allow evil men to lay their hands on Jesus. We seldom contemplate what it must have been like for Him to watch Satan manhandle His Son in the temptation in the wilderness and stir up wicked men to afflict Him and harass Him in every way possible. We don't often consider that when Jesus was on Calvary, God knew exactly where He was but couldn't rescue Him; He couldn't come to His Son in the eleventh hour and untie Him and comfort Him and protect Him as every father longs to do for his children.

Our sin has caused greater pain in heaven than it has on earth. No one has suffered more from its consequences than God has. Because of His great love for us, He chose to vindicate Himself by redeeming us, thus revealing Himself at the Cross to be the God of love and justice, of truth and judgment. "Mercy and truth are met together; righteousness and peace have kissed each other" (Psalm 85:10, KJV).

One day Bobby, a third-grader, looked down and saw a puddle between his feet on the classroom floor. He was horrified. He didn't know how it happened, but he had wet his pants.

Bobby covered the dark spot in his lap as best he could, and then he began to tremble at the prospect of being discovered. He knew that if he were found out, his life would be over. The other boys would tease him to no end, and the girls would call him a baby.

Bobby didn't know what to do, so he bowed his head right there in his desk and poured out a prayer from the depths of his heart: *Dear Jesus, this is an emergency! I don't know what to do. Can't You help me somehow?*

When Bobby looked up, he saw his teacher walking toward him with a look on her face that said she knew everything. He braced himself for the worst . . . and then a miracle happened. Susie was carrying a fish bowl across the room, and when she was passing in front of his desk, she tripped and dumped the entire contents of the fish bowl into Bobby's lap!

Bobby jumped up and shouted and pretended to be flustered, but in his heart he was saying, "Thank You, Jesus!" The situation had been completely changed. Instead of becoming the object of ridicule, he became the focus of sympathy and concern. The teacher sent Bobby to the restroom with a change of clothes, and Susie became the object of the ridicule Bobby had been fearing. When she tried to help clean up the mess, the other kids turned on her. "Go away!" they said. "Haven't you made enough of a mess already?"

That afternoon Bobby saw Susie at the bus stop. "You did that on purpose, didn't you?" he said gratefully, to which she replied, "I wet my pants once too. I know how it feels."

However trivial the story, we see the analogy to our salvation. Jesus spilled His blood all over us to cover our sins, and He took the ridicule that should have been ours. His sacrifice on the cross defines our relationship with Him, a relationship that we should always keep in mind whenever He asks anything of us—especially something we can't fully understand, which is the very thing that will cost us the most.

ENDNOTES

INTRODUCTION
FAITHFUL REASONING

1. Oswald Chambers, *My Utmost for His Highest* (Grand Rapids, MI: Discovery House, 1992), June 23.

2. Chambers, *My Utmost for His Highest,* June 3.

CHAPTER 1
CHRIST AND CREATION

1. McGrath, *Christian Theology,* 297.

2. Oswald Chambers, *Shade of His Hand,* in *The Complete Works of Oswald Chambers* (Grand Rapids, MI: Discovery House, 2000), 1194.

3. Claudia Wallis, "The Evolution Wars," *Time,* August 7, 2005, accessed September 20, 2011, http://www.time.com/time/magazine/article/0,9171,1090909,00.html.

4. National Science Teachers Association, "National Science Teachers Association Disappointed About Intelligent Design Comments Made by President Bush," news release, August 3, 2005, http://www.nsta.org/about/pressroom.aspx?id=50794&print=true.

5. Opinion, *Winston-Salem Journal,* August 7, 2005.

6. Elisabeth Bumiller, "Bush Remarks Roil Debate on Teaching of Evolution," *New York Times,* August 3, 2005, accessed September 20, 2011, http://www.nytimes.com/2005/08/03/politics/03bush.html.

7. Dan Agin, "Creationism vs. Sanity," *ScienceWeek,* January 23, 2005, accessed September 20, 2011, http://scienceweek.com/editorials.htm#050123.

8. Phillip E. Johnson, *Reason in the Balance: The Case Against Naturalism in Science, Law, and Education* (Downers Grove, IL: InterVarsity Press, 1995), 38.

9. Paul K. Jewett, *God, Creation, and Revelation* (Grand Rapids, MI: Eerdmans, 1991), 454.

10. Ellen G. White, *The Great Controversy* (Mountain View, CA: Pacific Press® Publishing Association, 1950), 522.

11. Charles Malik, *A Christian Critique of the University* (Waterloo, Ontario, Canada: North Waterloo Academic Press, 1987), 34.

12. Anand Shah, "Not Everything That Counts Can Be Counted, and Not Everything That Can Be Counted Counts," *Friday Reflections* (blog), October 11, 2007, http://fridayreflections.typepad.com/weblog/2007/10/not -everything-.html.

13. Paul K. Jewett, *Emil Brunner: An Introduction to the Man and His Thought* (Downers Grove, IL: InterVarsity Press, 1961), 33.

14. Will Durant, *The Life of Greece*, vol. 2 of *The Story of Civilization* (New York: Simon & Shuster, 1939), 362.

15. Ellen G. White, *The Ministry of Healing* (Mountain View, CA: Pacific Press®, 1942), 427.

CHAPTER 2
GRACE: ADAM AND EVE

1. McGrath, *Christian Theology*, 441.

2. Paul K. Jewett, *Who We Are: Our Dignity as Human* (Grand Rapids, MI: Eerdmans, 1996), 66.

3. Watchman Nee, *The Spiritual Man* (New York: Christian Fellowship Publishers, 1968), 2:64.

4. Ibid., 104.

5. Ellen G. White, *The Desire of Ages* (Mountain View, CA: Pacific Press®, 1940), 455.

6. McGrath, *Christian Theology*, 442.

7. Oswald Chambers, "How to Think About Sin," in *Biblical Ethics* in *The Complete Works of Oswald Chambers* (Grand Rapids, MI: Discovery House, 2000), 129.

8. Friedrich Nietzsche, "On the Blissful Islands," in *Thus Spoke Zarathustra: A Book for Everyone and No-one,* http://www.lexido.com/EBOOK_TEXTS /THUS_SPOKE_ZARATHUSTRA_.aspx?S=25.

9. White, *The Desire of Ages,* 300.

10. Debbie Elliott and Marisa Peñaloza, "BP Spill Psychological Scars Similar to Exxon Valdez," *Morning Edition,* NPR, December 1, 2010, accessed September 21, 2011, www.npr.org/2010/12/01/131694848/bp -spill-psychological-scars-similar-to-exxon-valdez.

11. Chambers, *My Utmost for His Highest,* October 5.

12. T. Marshall Kelly, lecture to the executive committee of the South Central Conference of Seventh-day Adventists, Birmingham, AL, March 7, 2004.

13. Sigve K. Tonstad, *The Lost Meaning of the Seventh Day* (Berrien Springs, MI: Andrews University Press, 2009), 58.

14. Ellen G. White, *The Story of Redemption* (Washington, DC: Review and Herald® Publishing Association, 1947), 50.

15. Ellen G. White, *Testimonies for the Church* (Mountain View, CA: Pacific Press®, 1948), 7:17.

16. Ellen G. White, in *Seventh-day Adventist Bible Commentary,* ed. Francis D. Nichol (Washington, DC: Review and Herald®, 1980), 4:1161.

17. Ellen G. White, *Selected Messages,* bk. 1 (Washington, DC: Review and Herald®, 1958), 366.

CHAPTER 3
BROTHERHOOD: CAIN AND ABEL

1. See White, *The Story of Redemption,* 47.

2. See also White, *Patriarchs and Prophets* (Mountain View, CA: Pacific Press®, 1958), 78.

3. Henry K. Lee, "Baby Found Dead in Garbage Can," *San Francisco Chronicle,* June 4, 2004, B5.

4. Robert Hanley, "New Jersey Charges Woman, 18, With Killing Baby Born at Prom," *New York Times,* June 25, 1997, A1, B4.

5. Watchman Nee, *The Normal Christian Life* (Wheaton, IL: Tyndale, 1977), 210, 217.

6. White, *The Desire of Ages,* 505.

7. M. Robert Mulholland Jr., *Shaped by the Word,* rev. ed. (Nashville, TN: Upper Room Books, 2000), 29.

8. Henri Nouwen, *Jesus: A Gospel,* ed. Michael O'Laughlin (Maryknoll, NY: Orbis, 2001), 133.

9. White, *Patriarchs and Prophets,* 71.

10. Ellen G. White, *The Acts of the Apostles* (Mountain View, CA: Pacific Press®, 1911), 37.

11. Ellen G. White, *Evangelism* (Washington, DC: Review and Herald®, 1970), 102.

12. Stanley W. Green, *The Canadian Mennonite,* September 4, 2000, 11.

13. White, *The Desire of Ages,* 678.

CHAPTER 4
HOLINESS: ENOCH

1. I've found Watchman Nee's insights on the body, soul, and spirit helpful; see, for example, *The Spiritual Man* (New York: Christian Fellowship Publishers, 1977).

2. Ellen G. White, *Testimonies for the Church,* 2:122; White, *Seventh-day Adventist Bible Commentary,* 1:1087; White, *Patriarchs and Prophets,* 85, 86, 88; White, *Gospel Workers* (Washington, DC: Review and Herald®, 1948),

52; White, *Testimonies for the Church,* 2:121.

3. J. Michael Kennedy, "Gentleman Bandit Turns Self in After 100 Robberies," *Los Angeles Times,* August 28, 1991.

Chapter 5
Salvation: Noah's Ark

1. Dennis Heatherington, "Operation Lifesaver," *MSC Health Action News* 14, no. 3 (March 1994): 4.

2. W. Robertson Nicoll, ed., *The Expositor's Bible* (Grand Rapids: Eerdmans, 1943), 1:16, 17.

3. Marcus Dods et al., *An Exposition of the Bible* (Hartford, CT: S. S. Scranton Co., 1903), 1:17.

4. Gordon J. Wenham, *Word Biblical Commentary* (Waco, TX: Word, 1987), 1:135.

5. Ibid., 144.

6. M. R. DeHaan, *Portraits of Christ in Genesis* (Grand Rapids: Zondervan, 1966), 87.

7. Wenham, *Word Biblical Commentary,* 1:174.

8. Ibid., 170.

9. Oswald Chambers, *Not Knowing Where* (Grand Rapids, MI: Discovery House, 1957), 29.

10. William Lane, *Word Biblical Commentary* (Dallas, TX: Word Publishing, 1991), 47b:339.

11. White, *Patriarchs and Prophets,* 95.

12. Environmental Science Services Administration, "Hurricane Camille, August 14-22, 1969: Preliminary Report," accessed September 23, 2011, http://www.nhc.noaa.gov/archive/storm_wallets/atlantic/atl1969-prelim/camille/TCR-1969Camille.pdf.

Chapter 6
Obedience: Abraham

1. Joel Osteen, *Your Best Life Now* (New York: Faith Words, 2004), 36, 56, 110.

2. T. D. Jakes, *Mama Made the Difference* (New York: G. P. Putnam's Sons, 2006).

3. Rick Warren, *The Purpose Driven Life* (Grand Rapids, MI: Zondervan, 2002), 297.

4. Ellen G. White, *Prophets and Kings* (Mountain View, CA: Pacific Press®, 1943), 55.

5. Ibid., 60.

6. Oswald Chambers, *Not Knowing Where: A Spiritual Journey* *the Book of Genesis* (Grand Rapids, MI: Discovery House, 1989), 4

Chapter 7
Judgment: Sodom

1. White, *Patriarchs and Prophets*, 156.
2. See Bernie May, *Learning to Trust* (Portland, OR: Multnomah Press, 1985).
3. Ibid., 161.
4. Watchman Nee, *The Spiritual Man*, 68.
5. White, *Patriarchs and Prophets*, 165.
6. Jewett, *God, Creation, and Revelation*, 247.
7. White, *The Great Controversy*, 557, 558.
8. White, *Patriarchs and Prophets*, 86.
9. Jewett, *God, Creation, and Revelation*, 384.
10. Ibid.
11. White, *Patriarchs and Prophets*, 522.
12. Ibid.
13. Jewett, *God, Creation, and Revelation*, 245.
14. White, *Patriarchs and Prophets*, 160.

Chapter 8
Sacrifice: Abraham and Isaac

1. White, *Patriarchs and Prophets*, 147.
2. Barack Obama, "Book Excerpt: Barack Obama," *Time*, October 15, 2006.
3. White, *Patriarchs and Prophets*, 152.